VIKING

Thames & Hudson

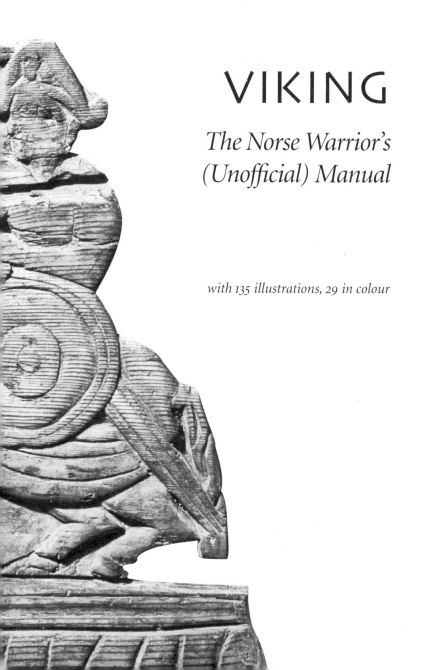

JOHN HAYWOOD

VIKING

The Norse Warrior's (Unofficial) Manual

with 135 illustrations, 29 in colour

John Haywood is an honorary research fellow at the University of Lancaster. He has written widely on medieval history and the Vikings. His previous publications include *The Historical Atlas of the Celtic World*, *The Penguin Historical Atlas of Ancient Civilizations*, *Encyclopaedia of the Viking Age*, *The Penguin Historical Atlas of the Vikings* and *The New Atlas of World History*.

COVER *Viking warrior ready for a raiding expedition.* © Thames & Hudson Ltd. Background photo © Paulmaguire, Dreamstime.com.

HALF-TITLE *Berserkers biting their shields as they work up to their battle frenzy. Impervious to the pain of wounds and positively eager to die in battle, berserkers are the most terrifying Norse warriors.*

TITLE PAGE *Norse warriors clash on horseback. This is something you won't see very often: Vikings prefer to fight on foot.*

PAGES 4–5 *Why we fight: a valuable hoard of hacksilver, arm rings and foreign coins.*

First published in the United Kingdom in 2013 by Thames & Hudson Ltd, 181A High Holborn, London WC1V 7QX

British Library Cataloguing-in-Publication Data

A catalogue record for this book is available from the British Library

ISBN 978-0-500-25194-2

Printed and bound China by Toppan Leefung Printing Ltd

To find out about all our publications, please visit **www.thamesandhudson.com**. There you can subscribe to our e-newsletter, browse or download our current catalogue, and buy any titles that are in print.

Contents

– 1 –
Why Become a Viking?

Remember that many a man lives but a brief time,
while his deeds live long after him.

THE KING'S MIRROR

× | × | × | × | × | × | × | × | ×

I t is Yule in the year that the Christians count as 991 since the birth of their god. The first snow of the winter fell two weeks ago and the nights are at their longest and darkest. But here in the hall there is warmth and light, companionship and plenty of ale, fine wheat bread, and roast meat for everyone. Most people are already drunk and on the high table the jarl and the Viking warriors of his *hirð* are boasting loudly about their exploits raiding in England last summer. About how they fought alongside mighty Olaf Tryggvason when he slew the proud ealdorman Byrhtnoth at Maldon and sent the English running for their worthless lives. About how the cowardly English king Aethelred paid them thousands of pounds of silver to go home. And how they'll be going back for more next summer!

Look at the warriors' fine clothes, and their heavy brooches and arm rings glinting in the torchlight, gifts of the jarl – but all of them paid for by the English. They've got wealth, status and respect. The young boys' faces glow with admiration; any stay-at-home fathers feel less than men and don't dare look the warriors in the eye. Not so the girls though, they're all trying to catch the Vikings' eyes. Even the slave girls, for once, don't look like they're pretending.

How good do you think it must feel to have your own place on the mead benches at the jarl's high table, your arms and fingers heavy with the rings he's given you? To know that everyone either fears or

A chief feasts his warriors at the high table while others serve them.
A life of privilege awaits the successful Viking warrior.

envies you? That the skalds will sing of your deeds long after your death when lesser men have long been forgotten?

If you'd like a piece of the action, read on! Here you'll find all the practical advice you need to become a successful Viking. But it isn't a career for everyone. If you agree with your father, that it's better to be a live dog than a dead lion, stick with your plough – you don't have what it takes. In our times, war is the most certain route to wealth and fame, but successful Vikings aren't treated like heroes for nothing. The price of glory is often a short life and for every Viking who returns home laden with gold and silver there is another who dies with a spear in his guts or drowns in a shipwreck. But what a life it is – what rewards and prizes for the daring warrior! What far-off places to plunder before the winter fires call him home! And remember, too, that the Norns ordained the day of your death even as you were being born and you won't live a moment longer no matter how far from fighting you stay. Don't wait for your fate to find you cowering in bed: *'eventually you will die, but glory never dies for the man who achieves it.'*

The Viking Life

Your best bet for getting to know about the lives and exploits of the great Viking warriors is to listen to the sagas. These are often about events that happened a long time ago, so don't believe everything you hear, but they're a great place to get inspiration:

This was how Svein used to live. Winter he would spend at home on Gairsay, where he entertained some eighty men at his own expense. His drinking hall was so big, there was nothing in Orkney to compare with it. In the spring he had more than enough to occupy him, with a great deal of seed to sow, which he saw to carefully himself. Then, when the job was done, he would go off plundering in the Sudreys and Ireland on what he called his 'spring-trip', then back home just after midsummer, where he stayed until the cornfields had been reaped and the grain was safely in. After that he would go off raiding again, and never came back until the first month of winter was ended. This he called his 'autumn-trip'.

What is a Viking anyway?

Have you been asleep for the last 200 years? A Viking is a pirate, a raider and a pillager. No one is too sure now where the word comes from, but it probably means 'men of the bays', maybe because that's where Vikings often lurk hoping to ambush an unwary merchant ship. Foreigners think that everyone who lives in Scandinavia is a Viking. That is understandable – Vikings are the only Scandinavians most of them ever see – but this is far from being the case. Only those who go raiding can by rights call themselves Vikings. Most people stay on their farms or work at their trades peacefully, hoping to avoid violence, though that's easier said than done in these turbulent times.

> **Tip** Just in case you're so dozy you don't know where you live, Scandinavia is the three northern European lands of Denmark, Norway and Sweden.

Why become a Viking?

'Poverty has forced them thus to go all over the world and from pirati-
cal raids they bring home in abundance the riches of the lands. In this
way they bear up under the unfruitfulness of their own country.' To
listen to foreigners like this Christian priest you'd think we are forced
to go raiding just because we are poor. If our land is so unfruitful, why
do we grow so tall and strong, eh? Fact is, the man wasn't born yet who
wouldn't like a bit more treasure and a bit more land. However, there
are many other good reasons to become a Viking; what's most relevant
to you will depend on your place in society.

King Ok, you're probably not a king. But every Viking should know
for whom he fights and why. Kings are top of the social hierarchy, set
apart from other men by their royal blood and descent from the gods.
Kings have been getting steadily more powerful for the past 200 years
or so, but they are still insecure. Although you're most likely to be a
king because your father was, in theory any man with royal blood can
become king. This is why succession disputes and civil wars are so
common. Kings must be good warriors to have any chance of holding
on to their thrones. They also need wealth to attract (and keep) a loyal
retinue of household warriors. This is the *hirð*: both royal bodyguard
and core of the royal army.

Kings don't have the right to levy general taxation,
and the income from royal lands and tolls on trade is
never enough to keep their warriors happy – you might
have noticed they have an insatiable hunger for jewelry
and fine weapons. Setting out on Viking raids overseas is a great way for a king to raise income from
plunder and payments of tribute, and at the same

*You'd look worried too if you were in this king's shoes.
He's probably thinking about how to keep his household
warriors loyal. Leading a Viking raid to plunder in
England might be the solution.*

time enhance his reputation as a war leader by winning glory in battle. Success breeds success: victory in battle attracts more military followers, leading to further triumphs and greater power (and subjects ever less inclined to rebel!). However, a life of constant warfare is dangerous and few kings get to die in bed. It is well said that a king is 'for glory, not for long life'.

Sea king Scandinavian kings are first and foremost rulers of men rather than territory. Because of this, men of royal blood can be recognized as kings even if they don't have a kingdom. All they need to do is attract a following of warriors – and keep them! Thanks to the charisma of their royal blood, this is not difficult. Leading Viking raids is a good option for these landless 'sea kings' – and if they get wealthy and famous enough, they might be able to seize a kingdom back home by force. Or, like the leaders of the great Danish army that invaded England in 865, which was commanded by an alliance of sea kings, they may be able to conquer a kingdom of their own overseas.

> *When Olaf Haraldsson first got a ship and men, the crew gave him the title of king; for it was the custom that those commanders of troops who were of royal descent, on going out on a Viking cruise, received the title of king immediately, even though they had neither land nor kingdom.*
> SNORRI STURLUSON, *ST OLAF'S SAGA*

Jarl If you're very lucky you'll be the son of a jarl. Powerful regional magnates, jarls are the pinnacle of the aristocracy, the highest men in the land under the king. The most powerful jarls, such as Håkon of Hlaðir and Sigurd of Orkney, rival their kings in power, wealth and the size of their warrior retinues, but of course they lack that special authority that only royal blood can bring. Jarls could once do pretty much whatever they liked, but now that kings have become stronger, they find this harder and harder. For jarls, therefore, leading Viking raids is a good way to increase their wealth and secure the loyalty of their warrior retinues as they struggle to maintain their status.

Hersir (plural hersar) This is an excellent place to start. With enough wealth to get you kitted up but never quite enough to satisfy your ambitions, you're the right stuff! Also called 'landed men', the hersar form the lowest rank of the aristocracy. They are local chieftains, with extensive family lands and many tenants and dependants, who preside over their district *thing* (assembly) and lead the local defence levies in wartime. Hersar are wealthy enough to be able to equip themselves well for war (you'll find out how to do this later) and they form the backbone of any Viking army. Hersar may own a longship or at least a share in one. By raising a crew from among their tenants and the local freeholders, a hersir can set off on small-scale raids on his own account or in alliance with other hersar. Or a hersir can take his ship and crew and join one of the big raiding armies under the command of a jarl or king. Most of the warriors in the *hirð*s of kings and jarls are hersar.

The growth of royal power has had a great impact on the hersar. Many have benefited from entering royal service, but their local authority has been undermined, limiting their freedom of action. And they're not quite rich enough to stand up for themselves if there's a conflict with a king. Most hersar just put up with this and treat Viking raiding as a seasonal occupation to get a bit more income, rather than a way to further any political ambitions beyond looking good at home. In the past, however, many who didn't like the way kings were getting a bit big for their boots went looking for opportunities to seize land and settle overseas. You'll have heard of the Iceland settlements last century – well, it was mostly hersar who led them, hoping to keep a bit more power for themselves.

A jarl (on horseback) and a hersir. Both are having their traditional independence undermined by the growing power of kings, but Viking raiding offers a way out.

These days, kings are less tolerant of freelance raiding and the hersar are now more likely to go to war in royal service. Though the rewards may be greater, many an old warrior feels nostalgic for the good old freebooting days when a man was his own master.

In Scandinavia, as you will know, only elder sons have the right to inherit land from their fathers. You might think it's pretty rubbish being a younger son of a hersir, but at least your father will have given you a decent military training and kitted you out for war. This gives you the perfect chance to be a warrior without too many responsibilities back home and you'll find lots of other younger sons in the ranks of Viking raiders, hoping either to win land overseas or garner enough wealth to set themselves up as a landowner. And of course if you join a *hirð* you may get some land as a reward for good service – tempted?

Freeman Well, you could do worse than being a freeman. The largest class in Scandinavia, freemen include craftsmen and traders, but most work on the land, as hired labourers, tenant farmers, or freeholders. Some wealthy freeholders have tenants of their own. All freemen have the right to speak at the local *thing* and are duty-bound to serve in the local defence levy. Most can afford at least a spear and shield – the basic necessities to become a warrior – and many will be a great deal better equipped than that. If you're one of the poorer sort, or a hired labourer maybe, you may own no weapons at all apart from the axe you use to chop firewood – not ideal when you're facing a mail-clad Englishman, I should warn you. Unless the local chieftain can loan you weapons you may never be required to serve in the levy, but will be asked to provide supplies instead.

There are many land-hungry men in this class who will gladly volunteer to crew a longship for his local chieftain, hoping either to win land overseas or win enough plunder to buy land at home. However, chieftains don't just choose anyone: they give preference to the best-equipped and most experienced men. So, if you're too poor to afford your own weapons, you won't get much experience in using them, so you won't be picked, and you'll stay poor.

On the other hand, if you're a craftsman willing to take the risks, tagging along with a Viking army is a great business opportunity – ships and weapons always need repairing. Same if you're a trader – it's rarely a full-time job and the line between trader and Viking is often a fine one anyway. Traders need to be armed for protection against pirates so they can also indulge in a bit of opportunistic raiding on their own account if they see the chance, while Vikings often turn trader as a way to convert plunder and captives into silver.

Slave (thrall) Tough luck. This is not a good place to start. You'll be a slave if your mother was a slave. Or maybe you didn't run fast enough when Vikings came calling in your neighbourhood, and you were captured and sold. Slaves are property and they have no rights. A master can kill his slaves if he wishes, sacrifice them to the gods or use them for sexual gratification. Despite this, male slaves are expected to serve in the local defence levy if needed and it is completely normal for slaves to be armed by their masters and ordered to fight in blood feuds with their neighbours. Not all slaves are badly treated and many are eventually freed as a reward for loyalty and good service. Once they have joined the ranks of freemen, some ex-slaves may have the opportunity to become Vikings, but most will probably settle simply for being free.

Woman A Viking career is definitely not for you. Women can become warriors only in the sagas about legendary heroes and gods. Though see below (chapter 7) for being a camp follower.

Women can't become warriors themselves, but what Viking isn't pleased to find a woman offering him a cup of mead back at the camp after a hard day's plundering?

Viking raids: the highlights so far

c. 789 Three Viking ships from Norway land at Portland in southern England. The locals think they're traders and come down to the shore to welcome them. Big mistake.

793 This is the one everyone remembers: Vikings sack the monastery on the island of Lindisfarne in Northumbria. The monastery was completely unprotected. The monks thought their saints would protect it: they didn't.

795 Vikings sack the Scottish monastery on the island of Iona and go on to sack another monastery in Ireland. Two more gangs of monks let down by their saints.

799 The first Viking raid on Frankia ends in tragedy: several ships are wrecked on the coast of Aquitaine and 105 Vikings are captured and killed by the locals.

810 King Godfred of the Danes ravages Frisia, part of the Frankish empire, and imposes a tribute of 100 pounds of silver. His warriors can't have been happy with the way he shared it out: one of them murdered him as soon as they got home.

c. 825 Vikings begin to settle on the Faeroe Islands. The only inhabitants – a few Irish monks – clear off sharpish.

The last sight many a monk has ever seen: a group of sword- and axe-wielding Vikings storming into a monastery.

A group of Rus (Swedish Vikings) are ridden down by Greek cavalry during an attack on Mikligard. Vikings don't always have it their own way!

832   Vikings raid the important Irish ecclesiastical centre at Armagh three times in a month.

834–37   The rich Frankish port of Dorestad is sacked every year. Nice little earner.

839   The first Rus (Swedish Vikings) travel all the way to Mikligard (or as the Greeks call it, Constantinople).

841   Norwegian Vikings build a fortified stronghold at Dublin in Ireland: it becomes a major slave market.

843   Danish Vikings become a permanent presence in Frankia after they found a base at the mouth of the Loire River.

845   Another Danish army arrives in Frankia: this one bases itself on the Seine.

859–62   Hastein and Bjorn Ironside raid in the Mediterranean: epic stuff, but they lose over half their ships.

860   The first Rus attempt to capture Mikligard is defeated.

c. 860   Gardar the Swede gets blown off course in the Western Ocean and discovers the uninhabited island of Iceland: settlement begins about 10 years later.

c. 862   Rurik founds a Rus kingdom at Holmgard in Gardariki.

865–76   A large Danish army conquers and settles swathes of eastern England: it becomes known as the Danelaw after them.

878   King Alfred of Wessex defeats the Danes at Ethandun (Edington), ending the run of Danish conquests in England.

882   Rurik's kinsman Helgi captures Koenugard and makes it the Rus capital.

c. 885   Battle of Hafrsfjord: King Harald Fairhair unites Norway.

885–86   Vikings unsuccessfully lay siege to Paris.

891   The Vikings get defeated by the Franks at the battle of the Dyle and there's a famine in Frankia too: the Vikings decide to try their luck in England instead.

892–94   The Vikings are given such a hard time in England by Alfred of Wessex that they give up and go home.

902   The Irish expel the Vikings: many of the refugees settle in northwest England.

911   Hrolf, leader of the Seine Vikings, is made count of Rouen by the Frankish king.

912   Alfred's son Edward the Elder begins to conquer the Danelaw.

912–13   A Rus raid in the Khazar Sea comes to a bad end.

917 If the Irish thought they'd seen the last of the Vikings they were sadly mistaken: the boys return with a vengeance and recapture their old bases.

919 Vikings under Rognvald conquer Brittany.

937 Athelstan, king of the English, defeats an alliance of Vikings and Scots at the battle of Brunanburh.

939 The Vikings get kicked out of Brittany, but there isn't much left to plunder there by this time anyway.

954 Another setback: Erik Bloodaxe is driven out of Jorvik and killed in an ambush on Stainmore, ending Viking influence in England – for the time being.

978 England's run of strong kings comes to an end with the accession of Aethelred the Unready (we knew it couldn't last).

980 Danes plunder Southampton and carry off most of its people. It looks like the good times are on the way back.

988 The Greek emperor of Mikligard founds the Viking Varangian Guard.

991 After Olaf Tryggvason defeats the English at Maldon, King Aethelred is good and ready – to pay tribute!

Tip You'll have come across a lot of new placenames in this timeline – and you'll meet many more as you read on. Take a look at the map at the end of this guide to get your bearings. There's also a glossary to help you out with unfamiliar terms.

OPPOSITE *If you go to join the Rus in the east, you'll often find yourself carrying your boat overland to avoid rapids or to get from one river system to another.*

– 2 –
Joining Up

To be called a king's housecarl is not to be despised.

THE KING'S MIRROR

× | × | × | × | × | × | × | × | × | ×

So, you want to become a Viking? Let's take it for granted that you're a healthy free-born lad, and that you're not afraid of a fight or a rough sea. If you're a powerful man's son, you won't be short of opportunities to go raiding: you've been brought up for war and proving yourself as a warrior is expected of you. Tough luck if what you really fancy is a quiet life, because you'll have no chance of maintaining your status if you can't lead men in battle.

If you're not high born, don't worry. All freemen have to do military service in the local defence levy under their chieftain, so, at the very least, you'll already have been taught to use a spear and take your place in the shield wall. Showing a bit of fighting spirit in the levy is the poor boy's best chance of becoming a Viking because it's the best of the levies who get chosen by their chief to join him on his own raids. The opportunities to become a full-time warrior are, however, limited and they are open mainly to members of the wealthier classes. Don't despair just yet, though – skill counts as well as class.

How is a Viking army organized?

All Viking armies are based on the *hirð* – the personal warrior retinues of powerful chieftains and kings. Keeping a *hirð* is expensive. The warriors of a *hirð* – the *drengs* ('lads') or housecarls – are very demanding: they must be housed, fed, clothed, armed and given frequent gifts of

Look out England, the Vikings are coming! A large Danish fleet makes landfall on the English coast. The masts and sails have been lowered to make the ships harder to spot.

gold and silver to keep them loyal. Even a king will not usually keep a *hirð* of more than a few hundred warriors. While the size of the *hirð* a man can support depends ultimately on his wealth, his reputation and birth also matter. You wouldn't follow a coward or a nobody would you? Warriors naturally prefer to have a successful war leader, and anyone with the special charisma of royal blood will easily attract a following.

Even if a *hirð* numbers no more than enough men to crew a long-ship, it is large enough to be considered an army in its own right. In Iceland, which, admittedly, doesn't have many people, even nine or ten armed men are called an army. But normally the full-time warriors of the *hirð* form only the core of a chieftain's army. When defending his territory against an invader, the chieftain has the right to call out the local defence levy as well. For Viking expeditions overseas the chieftain will reinforce his *hirð* by picking the best men from the levy. That's where you come in. Serving on Viking raids is not a legal duty like levy service, but that doesn't mean you can refuse to go. A freeman needs his chief's protection and support and he is therefore obliged in turn to support his chief's ambitions when called upon to do so. Usually, however, there is no shortage of willing volunteers to go on raids – you won't be the only lad hoping that this could be his big break in life.

Larger Viking armies are built out of these smaller private armies and sometimes number up to 5,000 or 6,000 strong. In the first century of Viking raiding, chieftains simply allied together to make war. Each chieftain remained in command of his own *hirð* so they all expected to take part in deciding tactics and strategy. The views of those leaders who had a proven record of success or who had royal blood always counted the most, however. All leaders also needed to take into account the views of their warriors because they could transfer their allegiance to another chief if they were unhappy with their own. Joint leadership might seem weak, but the big Danish army that invaded England in 865 had at least seven leaders and it conquered and settled nearly half the country. These armies could break up as easily as they were formed. Once a campaign was over, the leaders and their retinues went their separate ways, either returning home with their plunder, settling conquered lands, or joining another army campaigning somewhere else.

Tip Make sure you're noticed. All freemen have the right to speak so if you've got good ideas, voice them. A good leader listens to his men. And a clever Viking will be rewarded.

These days a large Viking army is more likely to acknowledge a single leader, usually a jarl or a king. Such powerful and wealthy men can maintain retinues of hundreds of warriors and can order their subordinate chieftains to come and join the royal army with their own warrior retinues. You might come willingly enough, hoping for rewards if the campaign is successful, but in reality you'd have little choice in the matter. To refuse would expose you to charges of disloyalty with all that implies – best avoided! The chieftains still lead their retinues in battle, but they are no longer equal partners in the campaign: they serve the king's interests.

Military discipline

Viking armies do not have formal discipline because they don't need it. The bonds of personal loyalty, mutual oaths and, above all, honour are enough to keep most men at their places in the shield wall. Honour is essential to a warrior. A man without honour is a *níðing* (nothing) who might as well not exist. The quickest way to lose your honour is to run away and abandon your lord and fellow warriors in battle. Most men fear living as a *níðing* much more than they fear death.

Levy service

If you're an able-bodied free man, you're duty-bound to bear arms and fight in the local defence levy. Even slaves may be armed in emergencies. Chiefs and jarls have the right to call out the men of their districts. Kings have the right to call out all the freemen of their kingdoms if they need to, but in practice they are much more selective than this. Levy service lasts only as long as the crisis. Most men are anxious to get home to attend to their farms. It may be the first experience you have of a real fight, but this doesn't mean you're a Viking warrior.

It is at the levy *things* that the chief selects the best men to reinforce his *hirð* on Viking raids or to follow him when he has been ordered to provide warriors for the king's army. This is your chance to get noticed. First preference is usually given to men from the hersir class. Though it is more common than it was for chiefs to loan weapons and armour to their followers, if you're one of the poorer sort of freemen, who cannot afford to equip themselves properly for war, you're unlikely to be picked and will be ordered to provide supplies instead. If the king calls a *thing* levy to raise an army, all freemen are legally required to attend with their chiefs. In practice, poorer freemen can't afford to do this, so the chiefs select only the best of their followers to go with them to the *thing*. The king chooses those he wants and orders the rest to contribute to the costs of the expedition.

Basic training

There are no formal arrangements for training warriors in Scandinavia. All freemen have the right to carry arms, so weapons-training mostly falls to family members. You probably can't remember the first time you were given a toy sword to play with. If your father took his responsibilities seriously, it most likely happened on the same day that you walked your first steps without holding your mother's hand. If you're lucky enough to have a wealthy father you'll have been given your first iron weapons when you were about ten. Yes, they were smaller and lighter than your father's, but you definitely haven't forgotten that day; it was the first time you began to feel like a man.

The amount and quality of training you'll have received will depend mostly on the wealth and status of your family. If you come from a family of poor tenant farmers, you probably won't get many chances to train because your labour is always needed on the farm. Your father will own an old spear, a shield and a wood axe, but he's rarely had the chance to use the first two. He might have fought in the shield wall with the levies or even taken part in a raid with his chief, but it's just as likely that his experience of war has been limited to providing supplies for others to fight. You'll have been luckier if your father is a *hersir*. He'll have all the war gear and he'll have led the local levies in battle – and maybe led Viking raids and served on longer campaigns under his king or jarl. He will have had much to teach you, but you still won't have got the training available to the son of a jarl or a king. With no farm duties, those privileged boys can train full-time from an early age with the finest weapons and armour and the constant guidance of the experienced warriors of their fathers' retinues.

Most boys' first weapon is a wooden sword. You can learn a lot simply playing the Viking with your mates. Though you won't get badly injured, getting hit hard with a wooden sword hurts enough to help you learn.

But don't waste time in envy – seize every opportunity to train, if you can't be as good as the best, you can still be better than the rest!

If you're not from the privileged classes, you'll get the chance to learn some military skills when you're old enough to turn out for the musters of the local defence levy. This is the time when the chief and his household warriors train the levies in shield- and spear-work and in basic tactics like the shield wall. In maritime districts you'll get to practise rowing and sailing longships too. Pay attention, show willing and be aggressive and you might get picked to go on a raid. In emergencies, it does happen that the first training some young men get is when the shield wall is forming up immediately prior to going into battle. Needless to say, this is less than ideal.

Archery training must begin in childhood if a bowman is to develop the necessary amount of upper body strength. Archery is a popular sport and it can provide something for dinner too.

Tip Getting involved in competitive sports, like wrestling, spear-throwing and archery, is another way you can develop and display warrior skills. If you show aggressive tendencies you're more likely to be encouraged than scolded. The famous Icelandic Viking Egil Skallagrimsson was only seven when an indulgent neighbour gave him an axe to kill an older boy who had given him a beating during a ball game. Egil's mother said she thought he had the makings of a real Viking and told her husband, a local chieftain, to give him a ship and some men as soon as he was old enough.

How old do you need to be to become a warrior?

You'll attain adult rights and responsibilities, including levy service, at the age of 15 or 16 depending upon the customs and laws of your district, but you'll probably have to wait a few years before being picked to go on a raid. The preferred minimum age to recruit a warrior is 18, when a young man is entering his physical prime. Most leaders prefer not to recruit warriors aged over 50 and, in truth, not many warriors live that long anyway. Younger and older men often do go on campaign and fight in battle, especially if they are of high rank. It is not unknown for men of royal blood to lead armies into battle when still in their early teens.

Joining a *hirð*

Most Vikings are not full-time professional warriors. They may be eager to sail with their chiefs on summer pirate raids or follow him on a longer campaign overseas, but most of them remain farmers at heart. If you want to become a full-time professional warrior, join the *hirð* of a chieftain or king as a housecarl. Thanks to family connections and better training this should be more or less automatic if you're from the chieftain class. Failing that, you'll need to have a proven record in battle before you're likely to be considered. King's men generally come from aristocratic families. This is partly for reasons of status; the glamour of being surrounded by the best blood of the kingdom adds to a king's prestige. Just as important, service helps bind their families to the crown. There is no great value for a king in recruiting a peasant lad of obscure family into his *hirð*, no matter how good at fighting he is.

A Viking warrior travelling on horseback. Horses are expensive, but once you've joined a hirð *you can expect the best of everything.*

If you do succeed in joining a *hirð* you will become part of a *félag* or sworn fellowship. All the warriors will have taken oaths of loyalty to one another and to their leader and you'll be expected to do the same. Oaths are usually sworn on sacred silver arm rings reddened with sacrificial blood kept for that purpose in a temple. These oaths last until death, but there are circumstances in which they can be broken without dishonour. In return for your loyalty, the leader has the responsibility to feed and house you well and to reward you with gifts of weapons, jewelry and land. If you feel that your leader is not fulfilling his side of the bargain, you're entitled to withdraw your loyalty and seek another leader.

As a housecarl you'll live as a member of your chief's household, eating and sleeping in his hall. Don't expect much privacy. Only the chief and his wife have a separate bedroom, partitioned off from the rest of the hall. You'll have to bed down with everyone else on the benches that are built into the sides of the hall. On winter nights try to keep as close to the hearth as possible.

Laws of the *hirð*

It was the custom that the warriors should sit in the places assigned to them according to their claims to worth, whether by seniority of age or by the higher nobility of their descent, so that the elders and betters took the more honourable places. Clearly, therefore, no man could be moved from his usual seat without shame and dishonour.

SVEN AGGESEN, *THE LAW OF THE RETAINERS*

If you're lucky enough to join a *hirð*, your fellow warriors will become your best mates, but they will also be your rivals. The warriors of the *hirð* are a competitive bunch, always eager to increase their status and reputation in the eyes of their war leader. This is as it should be because it encourages the warriors to try to outdo one another in their heroism in battle. Unfortunately, if one warrior gains status it will be at the expense of another. Because seats at feasts are allocated by status

– the most important warriors sitting closest to their chief or king – the increasing or decreasing status of a warrior is made plain for all to see. It can be a bitter experience for a warrior to give up his place of favour to another, so rivalries between warriors can easily turn ugly.

To maintain discipline and order, members of a *hirð* swear oaths to abide by certain laws governing their conduct. The laws of *hirð*s vary, but expect them to be similar to the following:

- Warriors can transfer their allegiance to another lord, without in any way impugning the honour of their present lord, at New Year only.

- Disputes between warriors are settled by the sworn testimony of two against one.

- Minor offences are punished by demotion of one place at the feasting table.

- If a warrior strikes another warrior of the retinue with his fist or wounds him with a weapon, he is expelled from the *hirð*, sentenced to outlawry and is given the shameful name of *níðing*.

- A warrior who betrays his lord forfeits all his property, is expelled from the *hirð*, sentenced to outlawry and is called *níðing*.

- The warriors of the *hirð* swear an oath three times in unison which binds them to try to kill an outlawed former member of the *hirð* if they meet him again.

- Any member of the *hirð* who does not attack the outlaw if he has the advantage over him of at least one man or one weapon, is himself sentenced to outlawry and becomes *níðing*.

Tip Check the rules of the *hirð* before joining – you might have to wait a long time before you can leave with honour if you find you don't like them.

Feasting

> *And when the army's leader calls the court to the hall, the jarl*
> *often begins to rejoice at innumerable men. Gift is ready for giving*
> *at the gold-breaker's feast, the company of people sits crowded,*
> *there is the greatest glory within.*

SNORRI STURLUSON, *HÁTTATAL*

Apart from battles, feasts are the most important occasions of a warrior's life. Feasts are not simply excuses to eat and drink to excess; they are opportunities for both a chief and his warriors to show off in public. For a chief, the ability to eat well, and to feed others well, is the most obvious manifestation of his power and wealth, so he will set out to impress. Expect to be served large quantities of boiled or roasted meat, boiled blood puddings, wheat bread, and ale or mead. Getting drunk is compulsory. Mead after all 'keeps back men's miseries'. Your ale will be served in drinking horns, which must be drained in a single draught because you can't put them down without spilling the contents.

ABOVE *A splendid drinking horn. Empty a few of these in one go and keep your wits and everyone will respect you.*

LEFT *Here's to victory! Vikings drink their troubles away at a feast.*

Tip Beware: heavy drinking at feasts is intended to test your
manhood. The man who can keep his wits when drunk is
respected, the man who can't is thought a fool.

However, as a warrior, what should matter most to you about a feast is not the food and drink, but where you get to sit. Feasting halls have two long tables arrayed on either side of a long central hearth. You can't just sit where you like at these tables: seating is allocated according to status. As a housecarl you'll get to sit at the high table. That's the one on the side opposite the door, with the people who matter. The chief sits at the centre of the high table and the closer to him you get to sit, the more important you, and everyone else, will know he considers you to be. As a guest on the high table, you'll get the best cuts of meat, the best ale and a personal serving woman to look after you. The less important people sit at the low table and those with the lowest status sit closest to the doors, with a cold draft on their backs all night. Stewards guard the doors to keep out gatecrashers.

Skaldic verse

The most important entertainment at the warrior feast is listening to the skalds reciting their latest compositions. The skald's profession is to compose praise poems in honour of kings and chieftains, recounting their heroic achievements in battle to enhance their reputations. Many of the warriors present will have been there in the battles the skald is describing and they know he's exaggerating and trying to flatter everyone, but it's exciting stuff to listen to. Poetry, like skill at arms, is a gift of Odin and skalds are also warriors. They know what it's like to stand in a shield wall, so their verses carry conviction. One of their duties in battle is to make up verses on the spot, providing a running commentary, showing off their own composure and presence of mind and helping to inspire their fellow warriors to perform great feats of arms.

Tip Make friends with a skald. They are good allies of the
ambitious Viking warrior. Those warriors who have performed
well in a battle are likely to get mentioned in the praise poems,
so their fame spreads and their reputations are enhanced.

One of the virtues the skalds praise most highly in a chieftain or
king is generosity. Skalds rely on the patronage of chiefs and kings for
their living, so that's no great surprise, but once a leader has been given
a reputation for generosity it's hard for him not to live up to it, so this
benefits his warriors too.

Skaldic verse is alliterative: the words have a strong rhythm that
carries the listener along. This rhythm makes a poem easier to remember and great verse quickly gets passed from mouth to mouth. Kings
and chiefs love this because it means famous deeds are remembered
long after the man himself has died.

A skald's praise for Jarl Thorfinn of Orkney

Against England the Jarl
urged his banner;
oft his war band
blooded the hawk-beak;
fire shrank the halls
as the folk ran, flame
ravaged, smoke reared
reeking skyward.

Through forts the famed one
went fearless to the fight-throng,
many a horn howling, but
high his banner.
Nothing weakened the warriors
of the wolf-lord; war
dawned then, steel dazzled,
wolves dined on the dead.

As skaldic verse is almost exclusively about the joys of slaughtering the enemy, the language could easily become repetitive. To avoid this, skalds make liberal use of kennings – clever metaphors for other words – especially ones related to seafaring and battle. You'll soon pick it up.

Useful kennings to know to avoid looking like a fool

• *shield damager*	axe	• *corpse beer*	blood
• *weapon storm*	battle	• *battle sweat*	blood
• *sword quarrel*	battle	• *sword's sleep*	death

Boasting

> *Let us call to mind those declarations we often uttered over mead,*
> *when from our seat we heroes in hall would put up pledges about*
> *tough fighting; now it can be proved who is brave.*

THE BATTLE OF MALDON

You'll soon find that warriors indulge in a lot of competitive boasting at feasts: it's an important way for them to reinforce or enhance their all-important reputations. Make sure you've actually done something before you have a go at it yourself. If you just turn up fresh from the farm and start bragging about your courage, people will simply think you're a fool. The trouble with feasts is that, once you've had a skinful of ale or mead, your mouth takes on a life of its own. When you wake up with a bad head the next day, it's no good hoping that everybody was too drunk to remember how you boasted that you're going to take on the enemy shield wall single-handed. That kind of thing always gets remembered and if you don't live up to your drunken boasting, you'll be dishonoured; if you do try to live up to it, you'll probably get killed. No one will sympathize with your plight. If you can't take your ale, it's best to keep quiet.

Tip No matter how ludicrous another warrior's boasts seem,
never call him a liar unless you want a fight. Insults to
a man's honour almost always lead to a challenge to
hólmganga.

Hólmganga

If you fail to stand up for yourself if you're insulted you will lose your
honour just as surely as if you had fled from a battlefield. You could just
kill the offender there and then, but this can get complicated. Legally
speaking, it's manslaughter. You'd have to pay compensation. Or you
might start a bloodfeud with your victim's family that could go on for
generations and lead to the deaths of people yet unborn. The legal way
to defend your honour against an insult is to call the offender out for
hólmganga ('island going'), a duel traditionally held on an island and
fought according to certain rules, in front of witnesses. If you kill the
offender under these circumstances, you don't have to pay compensation for manslaughter, but, though people do get killed, *hólmganga* is
not strictly a duel to the death.

Two scenes of hólmganga, *a duel*
fought according to strict rules to
settle questions of honour between
men. Losers pay the victor a ransom
– if they are still alive.

31

Rules of *hólmganga* vary from place to place, but there is always a marked-out fighting area. In Iceland a cloth five ells square (an ell is 3 ½ feet), pegged out at the corners, is used. A three-foot-wide furrow is dug around the cloth and bounded on the far side by a cord. If a combatant places one foot outside the cord he is judged to have yielded; both feet and he is judged to have fled. Anyone who fails to turn up is automatically considered to be a *níðing*, as is someone who flees the fight. Each fighter is allowed a sword and three shields. They agree in advance when the fight will be judged finished: for example, when the first wound is inflicted or when one party yields or flees. The loser, if he is still alive, must pay the victor a ransom of three marks of silver. In parts of Sweden, if you kill your challenger, you can even take his property.

Tip If you're unemployed, travel the countryside gratuitously
      insulting men so that they will feel obliged to challenge you
      to *hólmganga* to save face. Ideally, pick someone who doesn't
      look like they are any good at fighting, e.g. someone who is
      old or infirm or just a bit weedy. When they inevitably yield
      you can collect their ransom. Some out-of-work berserkers
      make a good living this way.

Defamation

One way short of violence to pursue a grudge is by composing short defamatory verses. Verses are easily remembered and are quickly passed from mouth to mouth, but – unlike the work of skalds – do their object's reputation no good at all. Good verses can long outlive the person they were meant to defame, and thus permanently damage their reputations. Because they know this, not everyone takes defamation lying down. Egil Skallagrimsson composed a bitter poem calling King Erik Bloodaxe a thief for seizing his property. The king wasn't amused and he swore to kill Egil if he ever saw him again. When Egil did fall into Erik's power after a shipwreck some years later, Egil used his skill at verse to save his neck by composing an extravagant praise poem for Erik. Not everyone is so forgiving. Defamers do get killed.

A formal way for two rivals to air their grievances about each other is by *flyting* at a feast. A *flyting* is a ritual exchange of insults. These can be very provocative, including accusations of sexual perversion or even cowardice, but they must be cleverly phrased, ideally in verse. At the end of the contest, the audience is asked to decide on the winner of the exchange. The winner drinks a large victory cup of mead or ale and then asks the loser to drink with him. *Flyting* is only for the quick-witted. If you can't think on your feet, don't try it – you'll only make a fool of yourself and no one thinks well of a fool. It's better to say nothing than something stupid.

Going berserk

Odin could make his enemies in battle blind, or deaf, or terror-struck, and their weapons so blunt that they could no more cut than a willow wand; on the other hand his men rushed forwards without armour, were as mad as dogs or wolves, bit their shields, and were as strong as bears or wild bulls, and killed people at a blow, but neither fire nor iron told upon themselves. These were called Berserker.

SNORRI STURLUSON, *YNGLINGA SAGA*

Berserkers are fanatical warriors who have been given special powers by the All Father Odin, the god of war: becoming a berserker is, there-fore, not a matter of choice. Berserkers form secret societies whose rituals are known only to members. Before a battle, they are able to work themselves up into a trance-like rage, howling like wild animals and biting their shields. In this state, berserkers have animal strength and ferocity and are completely immune to the pain of wounds. Because of this, berserkers usually fight without the encumbrance of armour, wearing only bear- or wolf-skins. Berserkers have a tremen-dous psychological effect on the enemy. Most rational warriors find it very unnerving to be faced by opponents who show such reckless

Berserkers biting their shields as they work up to their battle frenzy. Impervious to the pain of wounds and positively eager to die in battle, berserkers are the most terrifying Norse warriors.

ferocity and complete disregard for their own safety. Berserkers really don't care if they get killed: death in battle is the best thing that can happen to them because it assures them of a place at the mead benches in Valhalla with Odin.

Although they terrify the enemy, berserkers are dangerous to everybody. They may fly into an uncontrollable rage at the slightest provocation and kill or injure several people before they calm down again. Because of their reputation berserkers easily get work as bodyguards, but there will be a few in most *hirð*s. Unsurprisingly, a lot finish up as outlaws.

Join the Varangians

Vikings wanting a more formal military career than those offered at home can travel to Mikligard (Constantinople), the capital of the Greek empire. There, emperor Basil has recently created an elite bodyguard of Viking warriors. This is called the Varangian Guard, from the name the Greeks and Rus use to describe Scandinavians. Service in the guard is very well rewarded and the guardsmen enjoy a luxurious and privileged life in the world's richest city.

Vikings have always been welcome to serve as mercenaries in the Greek empire, but they were always sent to serve in regular infantry units. This Varangian Guard is the first unit created specifically for Vikings. The emperor Basil decided to set up the guard after his Greek bodyguard proved disloyal. Not being Greeks, the emperor apparently felt that the Varangians would be less likely to get involved in all those murderous court intrigues for which Mikligard is so notorious. The first 6,000 Varangian guardsmen were sent by Basil's ally, King Vladimir of Gardariki (Russia). Vladimir saw the guard as an opportunity to get rid of a lot of discontented Norwegian and Swedish mercenaries whom he had recruited to help him win possession of his throne and whom he now found he couldn't afford to pay. The Varangians were sent into battle almost as soon as they arrived at Mikligard, at a place called Chrysopolis where they defeated an army of traitors who were trying to overthrow Basil. Since then the Varangian Guard has never been far from the emperor's side. Basil is exactly the sort of leader a Viking

Rewards of a Varangian

If you want to see how good it gets, read about Bolli Bollasson. This famous Viking returned home to Iceland having served with the Varangian Guard.

Bolli rode from the ship with eleven companions. His companions were all wearing scarlet and rode in gilded saddles; they were all fine-looking men, but Bolli surpassed them all. He was wearing clothes of gold-embroidered silk which the Greek emperor had given him, and over them a scarlet cloak. He was girt with the sword 'Leg-Biter', its pommel now gold-embossed and the hilt bound with gold. He had a gilded helmet on his head and a red shield at his side on which a knight was traced in gold. He carried a lance in his hand, as is the custom in foreign lands. Wherever they took lodgings for the night, the womenfolk paid no heed to anything but to gaze at Bolli and his companions in all their finery.

LAXDAELA SAGA

Axe-wielding Varangians stand guard during the execution of a would-be usurper. Maintaining internal security in Mikligard is a vital Varangian duty.

should aspire to serve. He is a great warrior and very open handed with his Varangians. As a member of the guard you could expect to enjoy plenty of action and opportunities to plunder: they are reported now to be preparing for a campaign against the Saracens of Serkland.

Membership fees

Joining the Varangian Guard has to be seen as an investment. The journey to Mikligard is a long one: plan on it taking a year as it will probably be necessary to spend a winter in Gardariki on the way. The journey is not without danger, so for security you should travel as part of a fellowship with other aspiring guardsmen. You will be able to find paid work along the way by acting as bodyguards to travelling merchants or serving for a time as a mercenary in Gardariki. However, getting to Mikligard is the least of the expense. Applicants have to pay an entrance fee of several pounds of gold in order to join the guard. This means that in practice membership of the guard is only open to men of means. The Varangian Guard is an elite regiment and the emperor wants to recruit only the very best men. Appearance is important: the emperor wants to be surrounded by big, imposing men who will look both magnificent and intimidating. Applicants must prove their warrior skills serving in an ordinary regiment (for ordinary wages) before they are allowed to join the guard.

Varangian pay

Depending on service and rank, as a Varangian guardsman you could expect to be paid the equivalent of one-and-a-third pounds of gold a year, rising to two-and-a-half pounds of gold a year. This is far more than any other mercenaries in Greek service get paid. Even better, Varangians receive a much greater share of war booty than other mercenaries: the emperor receives one third, the Varangians together one third, and one third is left for the rest of the army. The emperor also makes generous gifts of gold or silks on special occasions, so you would soon recover the cost of your entrance fee.

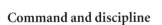

Payday. A huge hoard of Greek and Saracen silver coins. After a few years with the Varangians you could go home with sacks full of these.

Command and discipline

The Varangian Guard is commanded by a Greek officer called the Akolouthos. His rank is such that he is allowed to walk immediately behind the emperor in processions (this sort of thing matters a lot in the Greek empire). The 6,000 guardsmen are divided into 12 companies of 500 men each. The company commanders are also Greeks. Expect to have to parade regularly to have your weapons inspected.

Varangians are unique among mercenaries in that they alone have the right to judge their own members in disciplinary cases. Violence between guardsmen is punished by death unless there are extenuating circumstances. For lesser offences, banishment to serve in a remote garrison is a common punishment.

Duties of the Varangian Guard

The most important duty of the Varangian Guard is to protect the emperor. Wherever he goes in Mikligard, the emperor is always accompanied by units of Varangians. They are entrusted with keeping public order in Mikligard, guarding all the major public buildings and are always stationed in guardrooms by the entrances to every imperial palace. The Greeks are a disruptive lot for all their ceremonies and bureaucracy: there are frequent disorders in the city and riots between gangs supporting rival chariot-racing teams are common. The Guard also performs special security duties for the emperor, such as arresting

Varangian Dos and Don'ts

Do

- earn a few extra gold coins fighting wild animals in a spectacle

- try getting a tattoo like the Turks – lots of Varangians have one

- support a local chariot team

Don't

- yawn in a church service (however long and boring)

- practise paganism in public – this is the heart of Christendom!

- bother learning the language – there are translators on standby

- spend all your money at once; you should earn enough to have a good time and go home rich!

A Greek emperor, with a halo, on the road with a close escort of Varangians. Varangians accompany the Greek emperors (who don't really have halos) everywhere.

suspected traitors and torturing, killing or blinding them as required. They are also in charge of the grim Numera prison, where traitors are held until their punishment is decided.

When the emperor goes on campaign, some units of Varangians are always left behind to hold Mikligard. Those who follow the emperor fight as shock troops. They are usually held back from the battle to guard the emperor and are only committed when the fighting reaches a critical point. In camp, the Varangians pitch their tents around the emperor's tent: 100 Varangians stand guard at all times. When the emperor stays in a provincial city, the keys to its gates are entrusted to the Varangians overnight. Don't lose them!

Other Varangian units may be sent out from Mikligard to deal with minor rebellions or to garrison a particularly important fortress. Many Varangians are also experienced in seafaring, so they often serve with the navy, patrolling in fast galleys to suppress piracy. This is desirable work because the commander is entitled to a share of the value of any pirate ships he captures. Many Varangians are practising berserkers, helping to earn the guard a reputation for extreme ferocity in battle.

Varangian equipment

Varangians fight in the same way that Vikings do, with the same weapons: the broad-headed axe, sword and spear, so you won't need to learn any new skills. Viking blacksmiths have even been recruited to act as their armourers. All Varangians are provided with an iron helmet, a round or kite-shaped shield and body armour, either mail or scale armour. If fancier clothes are your thing, however, then this might still be the job for you: for everyday guard-duty, the uniform is sky-blue silk (that's right, silk for everyday wear!) with a gilded axe, hence their nickname 'the emperor's axe-wielding barbarians' (a 'barbarian' is anyone who can't speak Greek – it's meant to be an insult). On account of their heavy drinking, the Varangians are also known as 'the emperor's wine-swilling barbarians'. But what would you expect from people who don't know how to drink properly? Greeks always spoil their wine by watering it down. Unbelievable!

Life in Mikligard

There are too many Varangians for them all to be billeted in a single barracks. Look out for a billet in the imperial palace – here you will find spacious rooms around a pleasant open courtyard. These are the best: no more than about 12 men have to share a room. Other Varangians are billeted in comfortable civilian accommodation close to the naval harbour of St Marmas. Mikligard is not short of entertainment for off-duty moments and Varangians are not short of money to pay for it. The brothels are well stocked with attractive girls and there are plenty of exciting chariot races and other spectacles on the city's race-track. The city has huge numbers of taverns and, though there is no beer, wine is very cheap and it costs little to get roaring drunk. The effeminate Greeks look down their noses at this sort of behaviour, of course. No wonder they need to hire mercenaries to fight for them.

The Novice Viking's Guide to the Great War Leaders

Now tell me where to find the greatest Viking you know.

ARROW ODD'S SAGA

× | × | × | × | × | × | × | × | × | ×

Picking the right war leader to follow is the most important decision a Viking has to make. What a warrior needs is a leader who will deliver some loot and not get him killed. The best war leaders need to have good weapon-skills, know how to win battles and be physically brave – they'll set an example in combat that their followers can aspire to. Brute strength isn't everything, however. Low cunning in diplomacy and negotiations can be as rewarding as success in battle. All of this counts for nothing if the war leader is not also generous: if he's not, he won't keep an army for long. Learn what to look for from the examples of great Viking leaders past and present.

Olaf Tryggvason

Olaf's triumph at Maldon last summer has established his reputation as the top Viking commander of today. Still in his early twenties, Olaf is ambitious. Most people think he is raiding to build up his wealth and warrior retinue to make a bid for the Norwegian throne. It might all end in tears, but if he succeeds, the warriors who helped get him there will be well rewarded. Olaf is well known for spreading his wealth around and his warriors love him for it.

Olaf learned about Viking raiding the hard way – as a victim – and this taught him to be hard. He was the son of a minor king in Norway.

After his father was killed, his mother Astrid went into exile with the infant Olaf and his foster-father Thorolf. While crossing the Eastern Sea on their way to Gardariki, their ship was captured by Vikings from Estland. In the sharing out of the spoils, Olaf and his foster-father Thorolf were given to a Viking called Klerkon. Klerkon didn't think that Thorolf had much work left in him and killed him to save the expense of feeding him; Olaf he sold into slavery in exchange for a good cloak. Olaf was well treated and when he was about eight he was found by his cousin Sigurd, who bought his freedom and took him to Holmgard. Olaf was only nine when he killed his first man. It was Klerkon. Olaf spotted him in the market place at Holmgard and immediately split his skull open with the little axe he was carrying, so avenging Thorolf's killing. He is still a bad man to cross.

Since then Olaf's just gone from strength to strength. He stayed in Gardariki until he was 18, distinguishing himself as a warrior in the royal guard of the then crown-prince Vladimir (now king of the Rus). Feeling he was outstaying his welcome, Olaf left to go on a Viking cruise in the Eastern Sea. After plundering the Danish island of Bornholm, he wintered in Wendland. The next spring he raided among the Wends, plundering and burning, then rigged out his fleet and raided the coast of Sweden and the island of Gotland, routing the local levies. At sea he captured a Swedish trade ship, killing all its crew and seizing its goods. Olaf returned to Wendland, his ships weighed down with plunder. Later, he fought for the German emperor Otto against Denmark's king Harald Bluetooth.

This Viking has an inscrutable smile. Perhaps he's thinking of the riches won fighting for Olaf Tryggvason in England last summer, or maybe it's the thought of victories yet to come.

Two years ago, Olaf decided it was time to move on again. Fitting out his fleet, he sailed round to the North Sea and plundered his way south: first Saxony, then Frisia and Flanders. The wolves and ravens had plenty to eat that summer. Last year Olaf invaded England, sacked the port of Ipswich and defeated and killed ealdorman Byrhtnoth at Maldon. Byrhtnoth and his housecarls fought bravely – worthy opponents for Olaf! – but the levies were cowards and ran away. Rather than risk another defeat, the spineless English king Aethelred bought peace from Olaf for 10,000 pounds of silver. Now wealthy and successful enough to pick and choose his warriors, Olaf is wintering in Ireland and he's planning to raid England, Wales and Brittany next summer.

> *Olaf was stronger and more agile than most men.... He could run across the oars outside the vessel while his men were rowing the* Serpent. *He could juggle three knives so that one was always in the air, and catch the one falling by the handle every time. He could walk all around a ship along its gunwales. He could strike and cut equally well with both hands, and he could throw two spears at the same time.*

SNORRI STURLUSON, KING OLAF TRYGGVASON'S SAGA

PAST MASTERS

Ragnar Lodbrok ('Hairy-breeches')

If asked, most warriors would put Ragnar at the top of their list of the greatest Viking leaders ever. Trouble is, it's not easy to pin down who he was exactly. Ragnar was the son of the Danish king Sigurd Hringr. Or he might have been the son of Sigfred, the nephew of another Danish king called Godfred, who led some of the earliest Viking raids against the Franks in Charlemagne's time. It is also said that he claimed to be a

An old-fashioned helmet with face guard and a mail curtain. No smith has made anything like this for a long time, but Ragnar ought to have looked like this when he was ready for battle.

descendant of Odin. That's the way it is with everything about Ragnar. The Danes, Norwegians and Icelanders all have their own stories about him. It's almost as if the flattering skalds have mixed up the deeds of two or three different Vikings to create a sort of super-Viking.

According to the traditions, Ragnar became king of Denmark when still young and had to fight a succession of rivals to keep the throne. When he wasn't fighting them, he was raiding – absolutely everywhere, all round the Eastern Sea, Sweden, Norway, the Sudreys, England, Ireland, the Mediterranean and Frankia, especially Frankia. Ragnar used the rivers of Frankia as highways, travelling quickly in his ships to keep one step ahead of the Frankish cavalry. He defeated the army of the Frankish king Charles the Bald in 845 and sacked Paris, hanged over 100 Frankish prisoners to show that he meant business, and turned over the monastery of Saint-Germain-des-Prés on the Christians' most holy day, Easter Sunday. After that, Charles stumped up 7,000 pounds of silver to get rid of him.

Ragnar kept on raiding well into old age, he said, to keep his many sons in their place, so they wouldn't get the idea they were tougher than the old man and push him aside.

Ragnar married two, probably three times. His first wife was Lathgertha, who fought in Ragnar's army, only her long hair betraying that she was a woman. Impressed by her courage Ragnar went to her home to ask for her hand. There he was attacked by a bear and a huge

dog that guarded her. Only after he had speared her bear and stran-
gled her dog did Lathgertha think him worthy of her. This seems to
have rankled with Ragnar somehow and he soon dumped Lathgertha
for a Swedish princess called Thora. Ragnar received her hand from
her grateful father after he killed two giant serpents that were ravag-
ing his lands. The shaggy trousers he wore during the fight to protect
himself from the serpents' venom gave Ragnar his nickname, 'hairy-
breeches'. After Thora's death, Ragnar took his last wife Aslaug, who
was the daughter of Sigurd the dragon slayer and his lover, the Valkyrie
Brynhild.

Ragnar ignored Aslaug's warning that his ships were in poor condition when he set out on his final raid and he was shipwrecked on
the coast of England. This must have been around 863. Captured by
Ella, the king of the Northumbrians, Ragnar was thrown into a pit of
adders to be bitten to death. He warned his captors 'the piglets would
be grunting if they knew the plight of the boar,' meaning that his sons
would avenge him. Ragnar died singing about his heroic achievements
and looking forward to being welcomed into Valhalla by the Valkyries.
The skalds still sing Ragnar's death-song.

Ragnar seems to have had enough sons to crew a longship; no one
is quite sure how many and who they all were. But it was Ragnar's sons
Sigurd Snake-eye, Ivar the Boneless and Bjorn Ironside who the skalds
say avenged him, capturing Ella and killing him by cutting a blood
eagle in his back to honour Odin (see chapter 8).

The skalds may have embellished Ragnar's life, but it still has a
lot to tell us about the qualities that make a good Viking leader: his
bravery and physical prowess inspired his followers; he knew the virtue
of mobility; his attack on Saint-Germain, on a feast day when it was
least prepared, shows his tactical cunning; his execution of prisoners shows a calculated ruthlessness that strengthened his hand when
negotiating payments of tribute from a great king. At the end Ragnar
made a good Viking death, ensuring the everlasting fame of his deeds
and bringing honour to his family.

Hastein

Hastein is a great role model for any poor boy who dreams of becoming a great Viking warrior. The son of a Danish peasant farmer, Hastein was a freebooting pirate, pure and simple, and one of the greatest Vikings of all time. Unlike most of the Viking leaders of his time, he was in it for the loot not the land. Perhaps because he lacked royal blood, he never tried to conquer a kingdom for himself – though such a great warrior surely could have done so if he had wanted – but kept on raiding almost to the end of his life in a career that lasted 40 years.

Hastein began his career sacking a series of monasteries in Frankia in the mid-850s. He made his name when he teamed up with Bjorn Ironside to lead a fleet of 62 ships on a two-year Viking raid around the Middle Sea in 859–62. One of the stories that is told about Hastein is that during this trip he mistook the Italian city of Luna for Rome and, being eager to get his hands on the wealth of that legendary city, he decided to capture it. The city's fortifications looked impregnable so Hastein decided to gain entry by a clever ruse – Vikings love guile in a leader.

Hastein sent emissaries to the city, telling the townsfolk that they were exiles who were simply seeking provisions and shelter for their sick chieftain. Returning a day later, the emissaries told the townsfolk that their chief had died and begged permission to enter the city to give him a Christian burial. Completely taken in, the silly townsfolk agreed and a procession of Vikings followed their chief's

Eyes bulging with wrath, Hastein probably looked like this after he was told that the city he'd just sacked wasn't, as he thought, eternally famed Rome, but some one-horse Italian town called Luna.

A Frankish Monk Recommends Hastein for the Job of Viking Leader:

So much does this accursed and headstrong, extremely cruel and harsh, destructive, troublesome, wild, ferocious, infamous, destructive and inconstant, brash, conceited and lawless, death-dealing, rude, suspicious, rebellious traitor and kindler of evil, this double-faced hypocrite and ungodly, arrogant, seductive deceiver, this lewd, unbridled, contentious rascal, aggravate towards the starry height of Heaven an increase of destructive evil and an augmentation of deceit and through such accursed deeds is he more monstrous than the rest [of the Vikings] that he ought not to be marked by ink but by charcoal. He has defiled nations, flying hither and thither, he has claimed their wealth for himself and his followers.

DUDO OF ST QUENTIN

coffin to the grave at which point, Hastein, very much alive and fully armed, leapt out of the coffin and slew the city's bishop. In the resulting confusion, the Vikings sacked the city.

When he was told that he had not, after all, sacked Rome, Hastein felt so disappointed that he had the city's entire male population massacred. Unfortunately, Hastein and Bjorn got jumped by the Moors passing through Narvesund on the way home and only 20 ships made it back.

Hastein spent the rest of his career raiding in Frankia and England, skilfully combining violence, threats and diplomacy. He served as a mercenary for the duke of the Bretons against the Franks one year, and then extorted protection money from him another by threatening raids during the grape harvest. The mere mention of attack persuaded many Frankish cities to pay protection money. Cornered by the Franks while raiding in the Loire valley, Hastein agreed to leave Frankia, but in fact he just sailed round to the Seine and started plundering again.

Once, when trapped in England by Alfred of Wessex, he agreed to be baptized a Christian in return for Danegeld and a promise to leave the land. He quickly renounced Christianity and he didn't leave England either.

Only once did Hastein meet someone as tricky as himself. That was the abbot of St Vaast in Flanders. Threatened with an attack on his lands by Hastein, the good Christian abbot struck a deal: he would give Hastein free rein to plunder his poor peasants so long as he left the rich abbey alone. One–nil to Hastein. Hastein, of course, had no intention of keeping his promise, but the abbot guessed as much. After plundering the abbot's peasants as agreed, Hastein launched what he thought was a surprise attack on the abbey. The abbot had troops ready and waiting and Hastein beat a hasty retreat. One all. Even Hastein couldn't fool everyone all of the time.

Hastein was also masterly in spotting a good base. In the 860s he seized an island at the mouth of the Loire river and used it as a secure starting-point to plunder some of the richest lands in Frankia, using the great river as a convenient highway. Invading England in 892, he built a fort at Milton Regis opposite the Isle of Sheppey in north Kent on the Thames estuary. Hastein's fort controlled the main road from London to Canterbury and afforded easy escape to the open sea if things went wrong. When things got a bit too hot in Kent the next year, he simply took his ships across the Thames and built a new fort in Benfleet in Essex. Hastein always put great store in fortifications – the only one of his many forts that was ever taken by an enemy was the one at Benfleet and he was away plundering with the main army at the time.

Hastein was forced out of England in 894 and gave up raiding. By this time he was in his 60s, an old man. It wasn't that Hastein ever suffered a serious defeat at the hands of the English, it was that Alfred had reformed the defences of his kingdom in such a way as to take away that most essential advantage of the Viking raider – mobility. Alfred had fortified his main towns and garrisoned them, built a fleet of longships that were bigger and more battleworthy than those used by the

Vikings, and reorganized the levies so that he could keep an army in the field all year round. After arriving in England in 892 Hastein faced opposition wherever he went, making it impossible to plunder freely. He was wise enough to know when the game was up and he retired from raiding. He was last heard of negotiating with the Frankish king Charles the Simple on behalf of Hrolf the Ganger, leader of the Seine Vikings.

If the Franks or the English had managed to kill such a mighty Viking as Hastein, you can be sure they would never have let us forget about it. So it seems likely that he got to die of old age, quite an achievement for a Viking leader. Though Odin might've preferred his death in battle, he can't complain about the number of slain Hastein dedicated to him during his lifetime in all the battles he fought.

THE BEST OF THE REST

Erik Bloodaxe

Thanks to his blood-curdling nickname, Erik is one of the most famous Viking leaders, but he wasn't quite as great as he is often cracked up to be. He was lucky that he had good skalds, like Egil Skallagrimsson, to immortalize his deeds. Although Erik was a fearsome warrior, his career shows the limitations of brute force. Erik was a son of Harald Fairhair, the king who united Norway. He went on his first Viking raid when he was 12, not too young for a king's son. After his father died, he became joint king of Norway with two of his brothers. He showed how he meant to go on when he killed them both. Then he started on his subjects, who kicked him out and made his gentler younger brother Håkon king in his place.

Erik went into exile in Orkney and spent his time raiding round the coasts of Britain and Ireland until in 948 Danish settlers in Jorvik invited him to become their king. Erik could no more keep Jorvik than Norway. He was forced out before he'd had a chance even to warm the throne with his backside and King Olaf Sihtricsson of Dublin seized Jorvik instead. But the Danes of Jorvik didn't like Olaf any better and they invited Erik back in 952. This time he held on for all of two years before he was driven out and killed in an ambush on Stainmore. Erik's famous funeral poem describes his tumultuous reception in Valhalla: his reward for a life of constant violence. Unfortunately, too much of it was directed at his subjects and he forfeited their loyalty.

Erik Bloodaxe left more than a trail of destruction behind him. While he was king of Jorvik in England he became one of the first Viking kings to issue his own coins.

Halfdan

Halfdan, with his brothers Ivar and Ubba, was the original leader of the great Danish army that invaded England in 865 and conquered the three kingdoms of East Anglia, Mercia and Northumbria. It is said that they were sons of Ragnar Lodbrok. Halfdan brilliantly exploited the divisions between and within the English kingdoms. Landing in East Anglia, Halfdan forced the locals to provide horses for the army and headed straight for Northumbria, which was having a civil war. He quickly captured its capital, Jorvik, and killed both of Northumbria's rival kings in battle.

In 868 Halfdan invaded Mercia, but, for once, misread the political situation. Wessex sent an army to help the Mercians and the Danes withdrew to Jorvik. That was a one-off, fortunately, and no one helped East Anglia when Halfdan returned and conquered it in 869. The hapless East Anglian king Edmund was put to good use as a target for archery practice afterwards. An invasion of Wessex in 870–71 was repulsed, but Mercia surrendered after its capital at Repton was occupied in 873–74. Ivar died of sickness there.

The Danish army now split up: many men wanted to settle the lands they had conquered, others wanted to continue raiding. Halfdan took his followers back to Jorvik, which he made capital of his kingdom. His followers did well, settling on some of the richest farmland in England. Even this success could not keep Halfdan content for long, though, and he was soon raiding in Scotland and Ireland, where he was killed in battle with the Dublin Vikings in 877.

Ubba, by the way, also met his death in battle, in Wessex in 878. After so many victories, Ubba got over-confident and made the fatal mistake of underestimating his enemies. When he trapped a West Saxon army in a fort at Cynwit without food and water, Ubba sat back and waited for them to surrender. However, the West Saxons thought they'd rather die fighting than live as slaves and they made a dawn attack on Ubba's camp. Taken by surprise, Ubba and 1,200 of his men were killed. Lesson.

Olaf the White

Olaf was the son of Guthfrith, one of the petty district kings in western Norway (or maybe it was the Sudreys, who knows?). When the Danes captured the Norwegian base at Dublin in 851, it was Olaf and his brother Ivar who kicked them out again in 853. Olaf was a real entrepreneur and he built Dublin up into the biggest slave-trading centre in Ireland, maybe the whole of the north: merchants even came from Serkland to buy there.

Olaf was a good politician too, skilfully taking advantage of the endless wars of Ireland's quarrelsome kings, allying with one and then another to plunder widely. He overplayed his hand when he dug up the burial mounds of Ireland's ancient kings on the river Boyne looking for treasure. After that, the Irish tended to stick together a bit more, and Olaf started raiding across the Irish Sea instead. That's the great thing about Dublin: England, Scotland and Wales are just a day's sail away if it's not a good time to plunder in Ireland.

In 869 the Irish tried to seize Dublin, but Olaf defeated them and made them rue the day they'd tried: he sacked the archbishopric of Armagh, killing and capturing over 1,000 people in the process. Cleverly, Olaf chose to attack on the feast day of Ireland's most revered saint, Patrick. So much for the protection of the saints.

In 870–71, Olaf sacked Dumbarton, the capital of the Britons of Strathclyde after a siege of four months – a great achievement: Vikings aren't generally much good at sieges and Dumbarton is built on a very inaccessible crag. Olaf's reward was a multitude of prisoners for the Dublin slave markets.

Olaf's fate is unknown. Some say he was killed raiding the Scots, others that he returned to Norway to help his father against a usurper.

Hrolf the Ganger (Rollo to the Franks)

Because he was so successful, everyone wants to claim Hrolf. According to the Norwegians and Icelanders, Hrolf was the son of the Norwegian jarl Rognvald of Møre who became a Viking when he was outlawed by King Harald Fairhair. Everyone else claims that he was from Denmark, the son of a nobleman who was exiled after a dispute with the king. Either story could be true because so many Viking leaders have been the exiled losers of power struggles at home. According to the Icelanders, Hrolf was so heavy that no horse could carry him, which is how he got his nickname Hrolf the Ganger (i.e. 'walker').

Hrolf spent all his career in Frankia and eventually carved out a principality for himself. On account of it being ruled by 'Northmen', the Franks now call these lands Normandy. Hrolf arrived on the river Seine around 876 and took part in the siege of Paris in 885–86 and

OPPOSITE *Ships and horses are equally important to the success of a major Viking expedition.*

afterwards plundered in Burgundy. When the main Viking armies left Frankia for England in 892, Hrolf stayed where he was. It was a good decision: King Alfred was at the height of his power and he gave the Vikings a hard time of it there.

Hrolf gradually tightened his grip on the lands around the lower Seine valley. In 911 he tried to seize the rich city of Chartres, but the Franks defeated him. After the battle, Charles the Simple, the king of the Franks, agreed a peace treaty with Hrolf. He was granted control of the lands he had conquered and given the noble rank of count in return for agreeing to prevent any other Vikings sailing up the Seine, becoming the sworn vassal of King Charles and converting to Christianity.

One story relates that Hrolf was required to kiss the foot of King Charles as a condition of the treaty. He retorted:

> '*I shall never bend my knees to the knees of another nor shall I kiss anyone's foot.' Compelled, however, by the prayers of the Franks, he ordered a certain soldier to kiss the king's foot. This man immediately seized the king's foot and put it to his mouth and kissed it while the king was still standing. The king fell flat on his back. This raised a great laugh and greatly stirred up the crowd.*

DUDO OF ST QUENTIN

Hrolf kept the first part of the bargain: never since has a Viking fleet sailed up the Seine (though when King Charles died in 922, he did conquer a bit more of Frankia for himself, seeing as his oath wasn't with the new king). The Christianity he didn't take too seriously and, like many Viking converts, he continued to worship the old gods alongside the Christ. Shortly before his death he had 100 Christians beheaded as an offering to the old gods. Hrolf died around 928 and his son William Longsword took over his lands. His descendants rule them still.

- 4 -
Weapons and Tactics

*Learn precisely how to cover yourself with the shield, so that
you may be able to guard well when you meet a foeman.*

THE KING'S MIRROR

× | × | × | × | × | × | × | × | ×

The best war gear is expensive. Swords, mail shirts and iron helmets are only available to the wealthy or warriors with a generous lord. However, most freemen can afford at least a spear and a shield, and this is all you will need to be useful on a battlefield or a Viking raid. The basic skills of shield- and spear-fighting can be learned in less than a day and are practised regularly at the muster of the local defence levy. The better you are, the more likely you will be selected to join a raiding party, so keep at it!

Weapons check-list

Essentials

- Spear
- Shield

Desirables (in order of affordability)

- Battle axe
- Sword
- Mail shirt
- Iron helmet

A well-equipped warrior from England's Danelaw. Helmet, shield, spear, sword, axe and seax, he's got the lot.

54

Odin's choice

The spear is Odin the war god's chosen weapon. Odin's spear Gungnir ('swaying one') was made by the dwarves and always hits its target irrespective of the strength or skill of the thrower. At Ragnarok, Odin will use Gungnir to kill the monstrous wolf Fenrir.

Odin rides out to cause a bit of trouble with his magic spear Gungnir.

Spear

Taking his spear in both hands, Grettir thrust it right through Thorir's body just as he was about to come down the steps. The blade was very long and broad. Ogmund the Bad was just behind Thorir, pushing him on, so that … both fell dead, pierced by the same spear.

THE SAGA OF GRETTIR THE STRONG

Every young warrior dreams of owning a sword, but you will almost certainly start out with a spear and many a warrior will never own anything else. There are stabbing spears and throwing spears (or javelins). The purpose of both is to keep the enemy at a distance, beyond the range of a sword- or axe-stroke. Spears have an ash-wood shaft around 6 to 8 feet long (it is after this that the English sometimes call Vikings 'Ashmen'), with a leaf-shaped socketed iron blade.

Some spears, especially Frankish imports, have iron wings protruding from either side of the socket. These prevent the spear getting too embedded in a victim – you don't want to have to abandon it there!

A good collection of spearheads, including some fine Frankish winged angons. The wings of an angon prevent the spear getting embedded too deeply in a victim.

Throwing spears are designed so that their heads will bend when they get stuck in a target or hit the ground. This means they can't be thrown back by the enemy. Who'd want to be killed by their own spear? Another advantage is that this type of spear is very difficult to extract from a shield. The weight of the shaft drags the shield down and makes it very unwieldy. Another technique to prevent spears being thrown back is to remove the rivets that fasten the head to the shaft (best done before the battle starts). Any attempt to pull the spear out of the ground will result in the shaft and head separating.

Sword

Now Regin made a sword. He told Sigurd to take the sword and said he was no swordsmith if this one broke. Sigurd hewed at the anvil and split it to its base. The blade did not shatter or break.

THE SAGA OF THE VOLSUNGS

The sword is the noblest of weapons and also the most expensive. Because they cost so much, owning a sword immediately raises a warrior's status. The finest swords may represent more than a year's work by a blacksmith so it's not surprising that they don't come cheap. If you're a novice, you probably won't be able to buy your own sword and must hope to be given one by your chief as a reward for good service.

Choosing a sword

Look at the blade first. It ought to be between 26 and 32 inches long. A longer blade strikes harder, but a shorter blade will better suit an inexperienced swordsman as it is lighter and handier to use. Running down the centre of the blade should be a groove. This is called the fuller. It helps reduce the weight of the blade and makes it more flexible. Look carefully at the blade for signs of pitting or rusty inclusions that are a sign of impurities in the iron. The blades of older swords will have a herringbone pattern in the iron if they are any good. This is a result of the way they were made.

Creating a really good sword used to be extremely laborious. Because there was a shortage of good-quality iron, smiths made sword blades by pattern welding. This method combined rods of iron with differing qualities by repeatedly heating, stretching, twisting, folding and hammering to weld them together and beat out impurities. The resulting herringbone pattern is clearly visible on a freshly polished pattern-welded blade. Take note: the more complicated

RIGHT *There is no exactly right length for a sword: shorter is faster and less tiring, longer is slower and harder hitting. Choose according to your strength and skill.*

LEFT *The sign of a good sword. The complex herring-bone pattern on this sword blade is a sign that it has been laboriously pattern-welded to give it both strength and flexibility.*

this pattern is, the more work has gone into the sword and the better it is likely to be. Smiths often treated their swords with vinegar to bring out the pattern more clearly, so advertising their quality. Many of these fine swords are still in use and are highly desirable.

Some Famous Swords and Their Owners

Skofnung Made for the Danish king Hrolf Kraki hundreds of years ago, the Icelander Skeggi dug it up from the king's burial mound at Roskilde 30 years ago and found it was still in perfect condition, protected by its well-greased scabbard. It is now owned by Skeggi's son Eid. The sword is imbued with the spirits of the king's 12 berserker bodyguards.

Quernbiter As everyone knows, this is Olaf Tryggvason's sword: it got its name because it can cut through millstones (but don't try that at home).

Gram Forged by the legendary smith Volund, Gram was a gift from Odin himself to Sigmund, the father of the great dragon slayer Sigurd the Volsung. Sigmund broke the sword when he struck Odin's spear with it. The sword was eventually reforged for Sigurd by the dwarf Regin so that he could use it to kill the dragon Fafnir.

This wood-carving shows Regin reforging the sword Gram so that the hero Sigurd can use it to kill the dragon Fafnir.

Personalize Your Sword

Victory runes you must cut if you want to have victory,
and cut them on your sword hilt;
some on the blade guards, some on the plates,
and invoke Tyr twice.

THE LAY OF SIGRDRIFA

- Get the sword blade embossed with protective runes.

- Set a healing stone in the hilt. Wounds made by the sword will never heal unless they are first rubbed by the stone.

- Fit smart hilt and scabbard decorations of gilt bronze, or gold or silver if you can afford it.

- Giving a fine sword its own name enhances its reputation, and yours.

- Warning: handgrips made of ivory or precious metals look better than tarred cord, but will become slippery when your hands get sweaty in combat.

These days, improved smelting methods have made good-quality iron more widely available. Sword blades are now made from a single piece of iron with thin strips of hard steel hammer-welded onto the edges of the sword blade to create the cutting edge. These swords may lack the mystique of the old pattern-welded blades, but they are just as effective and much more affordable.

The final stage of making a blade is tempering, when the smith toughens the metal by heating it and then quickly cooling it by quenching in a liquid such as urine or blood. Swords acquire power by taking lives and it is said that the best way to quench a blade is to thrust it into the body of a living slave. Unless you actually saw this being done, you'll just have to take the seller's word for it: you can't tell just by looking at a sword.

A sword's hilt isn't just something to hold on to. Its weight helps balance the blade and it can be made to look good too.

The hilt is not simply a handle; it's an integral part of the sword. The crossguard protects the hand from blows while the pommel doesn't just stop your hand slipping off the hand-grip, it's a counterweight to help balance the sword. A good sword should balance just in front of the crossguard. The exact balance of a sword is a matter of personal preference, but it is essential to get it right. A well-balanced sword feels lighter and handier: a poorly balanced sword will quickly tire your arm in battle. The handgrip itself should be wrapped in tarred cord to ensure that sweaty hands don't slip in the heat of battle.

A sword should be kept in a scabbard when not in use. Scabbards are lined with sheep skin. The natural oils in the wool keep the blade clean and free of rust. Wear the scabbard on a baldric or a belt according to preference. If the scabbard is suspended vertically it can get entangled with the legs at inconvenient moments in battle. Suspending it in a nearly horizontal position avoids this embarrassing situation.

Many warriors carry a whetstone to re-sharpen their swords in an emergency. Ordinarily, however, re-sharpening a sword is a job best left to a blacksmith. An amateur can often make damage worse, for example, by making a notch bigger by over-grinding. Broken swords can often be welded back together by a blacksmith or recycled to make a superior-quality spearhead.

Imported swords

Vikings do not have a monopoly on good swordsmiths. The English and the Moors make very fine swords, but the best of all are made by the Franks. The top Frankish workshops inlay their swords with their founders' names to advertise the quality of their craftsmanship. Draw an 'Ulfberht' and friend and foe alike will know that they are dealing with someone who can afford the best.

But beware, dodgy weapons dealers know how desirable Ulfberhts are and there are a lot of fakes on the market designed to appeal to

OPPOSITE *A box of blacksmith's tools. Blacksmiths may only be craftsmen, but they deserve a warrior's respect. Where would we be without them?*

RIGHT *A sign of quality. Frankish Ulfberhts are the best swords, but beware of fakes. Real Ulfberhts have the name inlaid in pattern-welded iron: if the inlay is silver, the sword's a fake.*

status-conscious Vikings who can't afford the real thing. They may fool a lot of people into thinking you're a real warlord, but in battle they are likely to break or bend, costing you your life. If the inlay is made of silver, it is a fake: with real Ulfberhts the inlay is pattern-welded iron that has been laboriously hammer-forged into the blade.

As Ulfberhts are no longer being made they're getting hard to find. Ingelrii swords from the Rhineland can still be got new and are very good. Moorish swords are made in the warm climate of Spain and may become brittle, and snap, in a cold northern winter.

Axe

Olver lifted his axe, and struck behind him with the extreme point of it, hitting the neck of the man who was coming up behind him, so that his throat and jawbone were cut through, and he fell dead backwards. Then he heaved his axe forwards, and struck the next man in the head, and clove him down to the shoulders.

SAGA OF MAGNUS THE BLIND AND HARALD GILLE

When foreigners think of Vikings, they think of battle axes. The axe is the poor man's sword: a highly effective hacking weapon that is much easier and cheaper to make than a sword because it uses much less iron. Battle axes are designed differently from the axes used for tree-felling or carpentry, with broader and more curved blades. Don't be fobbed off with the wrong sort! The shape of the battle axe allows it to be used as a thrusting weapon, as well as for hacking, and also as a hook, for instance if you need to pull away your opponent's shield.

Two types of battle axe are common. The light handaxe is used with one hand in close-quarters fighting. It has the advantage that it is easily concealed behind a shield or under a cloak to give an unsuspecting enemy a nasty surprise. The heavy broadaxe is used with both hands. It is a satisfyingly brutal weapon to use, but it requires a lot of space to be swung effectively, so it's not so good to use in the shield wall. If you have the space for wide sweeping strokes, you can clear a

LEFT *Using the broadaxe two-handed, a warrior can clear a radius of 6 feet around him of all opposition.*

RIGHT *A fine collection of broadaxes. Thanks to its strongly flared shape, a broadaxe can be used for thrusting as well as hacking.*

radius of around six feet. It's a brave man who will step into the way of an axe wielded this way, no matter how good his armour, and it can easily bring down a horseman too.

A disadvantage of the broadaxe is that you won't be able to use a shield to protect yourself. Usually warriors sling their shields over their shoulders so that at least their backs have some protection. A disadvantage common to all axes is that their short cutting edges make it impossible to cut through both a shield and the man behind

The axe may be the poor man's sword, but its qualities are appreciated by rich warriors too, as the expensive silver inlaid patterns on this handaxe blade show.

it with a single blow, as is possible with a sword. The wedge-shaped cross-section of the axe head also means that an axe blow will not cut as deeply as the thinner sword blade. While a strong swordsman can almost literally cut a man in half from the top of his skull to the groin, with an axe he's unlikely to cut much further down than the neck. This is usually enough to give an opponent a severe headache, however. A final drawback to the axe is that its shaft can be cut through in combat. Try to find a shaft bound with strips of iron to prevent this.

Seax

He who has a little knife needs a long arm.
SAGA OF THE VÁPNSFIRÐINGS

Not very fashionable now that swords are easier to come by, the seax is a long heavy single-bladed knife used for butchery and close-in fighting – they're good for disembowelling people. There is a lot of variety in size and quality. Some have pattern-welded blades, but most are made as cheap alternatives for poorer warriors who can't afford a sword.

A good-quality English seax.
Its owner Beagnoth liked it well enough
to have his name inscribed on it in runes.

Bow

A short bow shoots rapidly.
OLD DANISH PROVERB

Although skalds rarely sing the praises of archers, the bow is a deadly weapon in skilled hands. Bows are particularly useful in sieges and sea battles, when it is hard to come to close quarters, and in the early stages of a battle before the shield walls clash. They can also provide something for dinner (try hunting wildfowl with a sword). Both long-bows and short bows are used. The longbow has greater range and power, but the short bow is handier for skirmishing.

Both types of bow are crafted from a single stave of seasoned yew wood. The ideal bowstave is cut from the radius of the tree so that two-thirds of its width is sapwood and the remaining third the heartwood, with the heartwood forming the front of the bow. This produces a bow with the best combination of springiness and strength.

> **Tip** Heartwood is clearly darker than sapwood so it is easy to check that a bow has been properly made.

Rain is the great enemy of archers. Bowstrings must be kept in a waterproof bag: wet bowstrings become slack. It is practical to carry about 40 arrows in a quiver. Barbed arrowheads cause the nastiest injuries and are the hardest to remove from a wound, but narrower leaf-shaped arrowheads give better penetration of shields and mail: carry some of both. Bows are inexpensive, but though easily acquired they are not easy to use. As a novice, you may find you are unable even to string a bow. Ideally, training for archery should begin in childhood to develop the best amount of upper-body strength – this is what the Ski-Finns do.

Archers with short-bows harass the enemy ranks in the early stages of a battle. Shooting on a high trajectory allows arrows to fall onto unprotected heads.

Shield

A shield is the cheapest and most useful thing to take to a battlefield. Used properly it makes a mail shirt superfluous. Shields are expendable – they're made to be hacked to pieces so you don't have to be. A warrior going on campaign needs to take at least two or three. The traditional Viking shield is circular, about three feet in diameter, with a flat surface. At the centre is an iron boss which protects the hand.

To fend off blows most effectively, shields are best held away from the body and tilted forward at a slight angle. Don't forget you can use your shield aggressively as well as defensively. The iron boss makes a handy knuckle-duster for smashing into an opponent's face in hand-to-hand fighting. The edge of a shield is used for prising open a gap in a shield wall by hooking it around the edge of an opponent's shield and pulling it away to expose his body.

How to ensure you have the best shield:

- Lime wood is considered the finest wood for shields. A rawhide strip around the rim increases its strength. More expensive shields are completely covered with leather and some may even have an iron rim. Leather-covered shields are well worth the extra cost because they last much longer in combat than a bare wooden shield

Only a wealthy man would own this much war gear – a fine iron helmet, a good broad shield and several swords, spears and axes.

- Painting a shield doesn't make it any tougher but does add a wow factor to a warrior's appearance and that matters when it comes to overawing the enemy. A distinctive shield also allows a warrior to be recognized in the thick of battle and get full credit for his heroic deeds. Come up with a really good design and a skald may compose a shield-poem in your honour. Dragons are bit old hat: try to use something that's got a story to it, like a famous deed of an ancient hero.

- Don't go for one of the trendy new Frankish kite-shaped shields: they're really designed for fighting on horseback and are less handy and give less protection than a traditional round shield when fighting on foot.

The worst thing that can happen to a shield is for a spear to get stuck in it. This makes a shield heavy and very unwieldy. If you can't get the spear out quickly you're better off throwing your shield away, but then you've lost your first (and perhaps only) line of defence.

If you've lost your shield, wrapping a cloak thickly around your shield arm offers some protection against blows.

Mail shirt

Very expensive, very effective, a mail shirt, or byrnie, will save you an arm and a leg. Mail is made from rings of wrought-iron wire, each of which must be hammer welded or riveted closed. Twenty- to thirty-thousand rings are needed to make a byrnie, so this is quite an investment.

Mail lasts a long time (generations sometimes) and battle damage can be patched relatively easily by a skilled blacksmith, so there are plenty of byrnies around in the armouries of the powerful. They are, of course, also highly desirable war booty and one of the first things to strip from the dead. Check a byrnie carefully. Make sure that any repairs have been carried out competently and, especially if it's an old one, make sure that the rings are not worn so thin as to be useless.

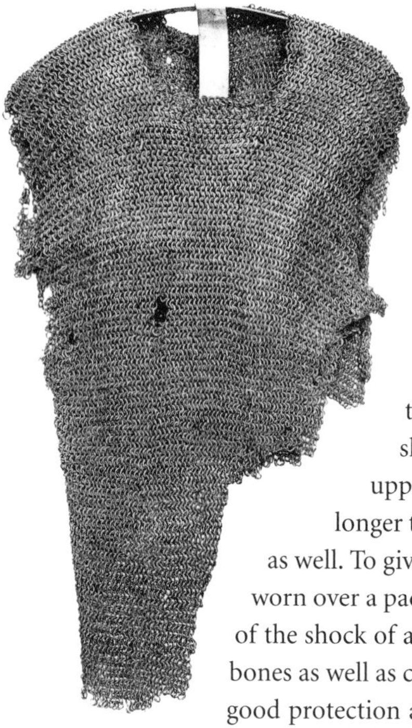

This mail shirt has been in a tough battle and needs to be sent to a good blacksmith. After repair it will be as strong as ever, which is more than could be said for an unprotected human body that had taken that kind of a battering.

It should be at least long enough to cover the groin and the sleeves should be long enough to cover the upper arm. Newer byrnies tend to be longer than older ones and cover the thighs as well. To give the best protection, mail has to be worn over a padded jacket, which will absorb some of the shock of a blow and protect you from broken bones as well as cuts. Though don't forget: mail gives good protection against slashing injuries, but is vulnerable to arrows and well-placed spear thrusts.

A byrnie weighs in at a hefty 26 pounds or more. Despite this they are very flexible and surprisingly comfortable to wear (except in hot weather), though the weight falls mainly on the shoulders. Tightly

Approximate Prices of Weapons in Silver

Spear – 1½ ounces

Sword – 4 to 60 ounces depending on quality

Helmet – 13 ounces

Mail byrnie – 26 ounces

fastening a belt around the shirt relieves the burden on the shoulders by transferring some of the weight to the hips.

How to care for your mail shirt:

- When properly patched, damaged mail is as strong as it was before.

- Wrought iron does not rust easily, but mail, like anything else made of iron, still needs to be protected from damp. Don't put it away wet and forget about it until the next campaigning season.

- Mail is easy to clean. Really. Just roll your byrnie in a barrel of sand to remove rust. Or grease it and wear it – any rust will come off as the links rub together.

Helmet

Like mail, iron helmets are very expensive: most warriors will go into battle bare-headed or with only a padded leather cap for protection. The helmets made these days usually have a simple conical shape. They may be made from a single sheet of iron, but more often they are made by riveting smaller iron sheets into an iron frame. Better-quality helmets have an iron noseguard riveted onto the front and an aventail (a mail curtain) fastened to the rear for neck protection.

An iron helmet with a faceplate. The faceplate makes for a fierce appearance, but it tends to direct spear- and sword-thrusts into the eyes. For this reason, this type of helmet is rarely seen these days – a simple noseguard is more effective.

A helmet must be well padded to absorb the shock of a blow (an unpadded helmet is just a skull-crusher) and not too tight. Older helmets sometimes have cheek-guards. These do protect the face, but they are uncomfortable and make it difficult to hear. In battle that can be a disadvantage. Another feature found on some older helmets is an iron faceplate with holes to see through. This will give you a fierce expression and is supposed to protect the face. In practice this can simply divert spear and sword thrusts into the eye holes, which is not what you want at all.

Helmets weigh about four pounds and are quite comfortable: if you're lucky enough to own a helmet, it's a good idea to wear it all the time when on the march in hostile territory and not only when you're expecting a battle.

Weak spots

Helmet, mail and shield give good protection on the battlefield, but don't go thinking you can't get hurt. Your face, especially your eyes, your lower arms and hands, and your legs and feet are all vulnerable. Your enemies know this. Leg wounds are the most dangerous: if you finish up on the ground, a spear in the face or up the arse will quickly kill you no matter how good your armour is. If you don't get trampled to death first.

A heavily armoured warrior has a clear advantage in the shield wall, but in skirmishing a man fighting without armour is faster and more agile, so the odds are more even.

Battle formations

Vikings do not go in for complicated battlefield manoeuvres, but then neither do most of our opponents. We employ just one basic formation – the shield wall – which can be mastered by novices with very little training. You'll pick it up in no time. Although Vikings put a high value on individual heroics, the good warrior knows that he must not

Mail-clad warriors formed up and under attack in a shield wall. The warriors are using their spears overarm to avoid exposing their bodies when thrusting at the enemy.

allow his thirst for personal fame and glory to endanger the success of the army as a whole. Maintaining a battle formation requires self-discipline and team work.

Shield wall The name says it all. The warriors form up in a continuous line, close enough to one another that their shields overlap slightly and form a continuous wall, but not so close that they cannot move and use their weapons freely. Ideally the wall should be about four ranks deep. In battle, the men at the rear move forward to replace the fallen and add weight to the formation for the pushing and shoving that goes on when two shield walls are locked in combat. The commander positions himself in the front rank at the centre, with his standard bearer alongside him. The shield wall can be used for attack as well as defence. When attacking the enemy's shield wall, try to keep in as close formation as possible: hopefully your sheer momentum will break or disorganize it.

Swine-wedge The swine-wedge (*svinfylking*) tactic was invented by Odin. Warriors assemble in a wedge-shaped formation with the aim of punching a hole through the enemy's shield wall by applying an overwhelming weight of numbers at one point. Warriors on the left-hand side of the formation get the protection of their shields, those on the right have their flanks exposed (it is not usual to change the shield to the right hand because this means using the sword, spear, or axe in the weaker left hand). So try to be on the left. Shortly before contact, concentrate all javelins against the part of the shield wall you are trying to break. Then press on with lowered spears. Forming a swine-wedge in the heat of battle is very difficult and in practice the formation is rarely used. The way to counter a swine-wedge is to form the shield wall into an arc or reverse 'V' shape so that the tip of the swine-wedge is enveloped as soon as it makes contact.

Shield-burg In this formation a small group of warriors use their shields to create a 'fortress' that protects them from attack from all sides and from missiles raining down on them from above. If you're on the edge of the formation, use your shield in the same way as in a shield wall, but if you're in the middle hold your shield over your head to help make a roof of overlapping shields. The shield-burg is not very useful on the battlefield because it is hard to hold the formation on the move. It is most useful when attacking the walls or gates of a fort or city.

– 5 –
Going to Sea

On the sea you must be alert and fearless.... Keep your ship attractive,
for then capable men will join you and it will be well manned.

THE KING'S MIRROR

× | × | × | × | × | × | × | × | ×

If you want to be a Viking you'll need to be a sailor as well as a warrior. Scandinavia is almost surrounded by the sea, so Viking raids would be impossible without ships and the skills to sail them. Shipbuilding and navigation are specialized crafts, acquired only by years of experience, but all Vikings need to be able to row, help sail a ship if needed and fight as well at sea as they do on land. If you aspire one day to lead Viking raids you need to acquire some knowledge of navigation and sea conditions. Even if you don't, you still need to be able to keep yourself and your gear dry when at sea and help prepare a ship for battle.

A longship under sail in fair weather and everyone looks happy and relaxed. But it's not always like this: the sea can be a Viking's most dangerous enemy.

Ships are more than a means of transport, they're what give us the edge over our opponents. Ships allow raiding parties to descend almost anywhere on a hostile coast with little warning and quickly penetrate far inland on navigable rivers. Travel by sea is risky, but it's much faster than travel by land: 165 miles is considered an average day's sail – try riding that distance in a day on a horse! If raiders meet resistance at one landing place, they can sail away and make a landing somewhere else long before land-based defenders have a chance to catch up with them.

Ships

[Cnut the Great] had a dragon-ship so large that it had sixty benches of
rowers, and the figurehead was gilt all over.... The sails [had] stripes
of blue, red and green, and the vessel [was] painted all
above the waterline.

ST OLAF'S SAGA

Visit any Scandinavian port or trading place and you'll see ships of all types and sizes moored to jetties or hauled up on the beach, from small fishing boats for two or four oarsmen and slender *byrdings* (coasters) to broad-beamed *knarrs* (long-distance traders) and sleek longships.

Traders' knarrs and byrdings are prey for a Viking, but snekkes and drakkars
will be full of warriors, so treat as potentially hostile till you know who's aboard.

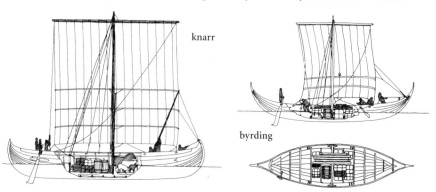

knarr

byrding

The ships most used for war are the longships. There are two main types, *snekkes* (snakes) and *drakkars* (dragons). If you were brought up in a coastal district you'll have been familiar with snekkes from childhood as these are the kind of ships owned by local chieftains for their private raids and for the use of the local defence levies. Long and narrow, snekkes vary from around 55 to 70 feet in length and have crews of between 24 and 36 oarsmen.

Snekkes are ideal ships for strandhogg (see chapter 8) and other small-scale hit-and-run expeditions. Their long, narrow hulls make them fast under sail or oars and they draw only about 18 inches of water fully loaded, so they can be run very close inshore or up even quite minor rivers without running aground. The snekkes used by the levy fleets are very basic. Local peasants have to provide the materials as part of their duties to their chief or king and will usually use the cheapest wood they can get away with, including second-hand timbers from old ships.

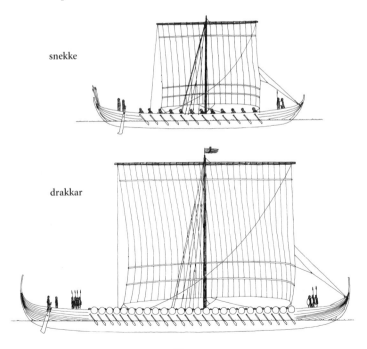

snekke

drakkar

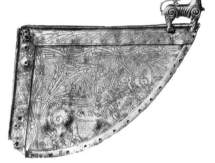

RIGHT *A gilded weathervane atop the mast finishes a ship off beautifully and tells you from which direction the wind is blowing too. If you can't afford one, don't despair – a flag will do the same job for a fraction of the cost.*

BELOW *Like anything expensive, ships are status symbols. Kings and jarls like lavish decorations on their ships so that no one can possibly mistake them for a run-of-the-mill levy ship.*

Drakkars are just as much symbols of authority and wealth as being war and transport ships. These enormous longships are so costly that only jarls and kings can afford them. No expense is spared when fitting out a drakkar with carved figureheads and brightly painted hulls, gilded weathervanes, multi-coloured sails, and embroidered pennants, to make it create a truly magnificent impression. Drakkars are anything from 100 to 120 feet long and they tower over a snekke. They have crews of 60 to 80 oarsmen and because of their size they can carry as many as 500 warriors on a short voyage.

All this means one drakkar can comfortably take on half-a-dozen snekkes in a sea fight. Their size also makes drakkars a more stable fighting platform than snekkes, especially in a choppy sea. They can even sail in rougher conditions without the risk of swamping. Because of their greater draught, drakkars are not suitable for strandhogg but, then, the men who own them are after bigger prizes than a few cows or some peasants for the slave market.

A third type of ship that can be used for raiding, travel and trade is the *karve*. Karves carry a full crew of 30 to 36 oarsmen and are about the same length as a snekke but the proportions of their hulls are more like those of a trade ship than a longship, being quite broad. These ships are more seaworthy than a snekke, and can carry about twice as many men as a snekke of similar length, but are not as fast under either oars or sails. They are used mainly by the Norwegians, and by the Rus (who call them *korabis*), whose trade ships need large crews for portages (see below) and for defence against ambushes.

Command

The captain of a ship is the steersman (or helmsman). He is usually the owner of the ship rather than the most experienced sailor. As steersman, he will deputize the day-to-day running of the ship to the skipper, who usually will have been chosen for his knowledge of seafaring and navigation. In a longship setting out on a raiding expedition, the skipper may be the only professional seaman. If the local chieftain who owns the ship is steersman, his warriors will be the crew.

Tip Try to find a ship with a skipper who has a personal knowledge of the seas over which the raiding ship is to pass.

A steersman stands in the stern of his longship while the crew adjust the rigging. Sailing a ship requires teamwork.

Life on board ship

I have endured cruel anxiety at heart and experienced many anxious
lodging-places afloat, and the terrible surging of the waves.... My feet
were pinched by the cold, shackled by the frost in cold chains, while
anxieties sighed hot around my heart. Hunger tore from within
at the mind of one wearied by the ocean.

THE SEAFARER

In fine summer weather, sailing with a following breeze is seductively enjoyable. Just as the skalds describe it, the ship speeds over the whale's road like a sea-stallion. Everyone is full of optimism, looking forward to a successful raid or a glorious homecoming with a chest full of plunder. Most nights the ship will drop anchor in a sheltered bay or inlet. If it's hostile territory, everyone will sleep on board the ship for

LEFT *A typically simple Viking anchor: a rock between a forked branch, held in place by the wooden flukes. The flukes dig into the sea bed, holding the ship fast.*

BELOW *The ship is your home for as long as the voyage takes, so you'll need to take a full set of domestic utensils such as water butts, buckets, ladles, mixing troughs, cutting boards, kitchen knives and all the rest of it.*

safety under an awning that can be rigged over the deck for shelter. It's not exactly comfortable. A longship with a full crew is pretty crowded and you just have to find space to sleep on the deck between sea chests, water barrels and all the other clutter. Many ships have a small hearth so there's a chance of getting some hot porridge to eat. Otherwise, food at sea is mainly bread and butter, and dried fish. Make sure your final meal on dry land has all your favourite dishes – it'll be a while before you get such food again!

Sailing in bad weather is quite another story. Viking ships are completely open to the elements and it's often not possible to erect an awning over the deck for shelter in bad weather when at sea. The awnings catch the wind and make a ship difficult to steer, so you just have to put up with being wet and cold for as long as the bad weather lasts. No fires can be lit so, just when you want it most, there is no hot food to warm the belly. If you're an inexperienced sailor, you won't be bothered by the cold, the wet, or the lack of hot food: you'll be too seasick to care whether you live or die. In summer these conditions are merely miserable, but in winter they can quickly become fatal.

> Tip Salt water rusts iron far quicker than rain. In preparation for
> a voyage, grease all weapons and armour well and store them
> in your sea chest inside a waterproof sealskin bag. Make sure
> that the weapons are the last thing to be packed. There are
> pirates all over the place these days so you never know when
> you might need to defend yourself. The sea chest is also your
> rowing bench.

Navigation

Navigation is not an exact art: even experienced seafarers can suffer from *hafvilla*, that is completely losing their bearings out at sea. This is most likely to happen if a ship is becalmed for a long period in poor visibility when it may drift imperceptibly far off its course on the ocean currents.

Navigation Aids

Sun stone This is a clear crystal that is found in Iceland and Norway. The stone can reveal the position of the sun even when the sky is completely clouded over. The navigator looks at the sky through the crystal, which changes colour if it is pointed in the direction of the sun. Despite being well known, it is strangely difficult to find anyone who has actually used one.

Sounding line This is a rope with a lead weight on the end that is lowered from a ship into the sea to measure its depth. This is an English practice that is gradually becoming accepted by Viking navigators, especially in the Baltic. The English like to keep about 10 fathoms (60 feet) of water under their keels when coasting.

Where possible, skippers simply follow the coast, keeping a safe distance offshore to avoid shoals and reefs, and navigating using landmarks on shore. Anything longer than an overnight voyage out of sight of land is avoided when possible. In good conditions, it takes only two or three days to cross the North Sea from Denmark to England, but this is rarely done. Danish raiding fleets gather in the sheltered Limfjord in northern Jutland. From there they enter the North Sea and head south along the coasts of Jutland, Germany, Frisia and Flanders to the narrow seas before crossing to Kent and following the English coast west or north to the intended destination. In the Eastern Sea you'll never need to sail out of sight of land.

Beware of coastal sailing at night: because of the risk of grounding, seek out a sheltered anchorage before darkness falls and resume the voyage in the morning. Only the Norwegians make regular open-sea voyages, sailing direct across the North Sea to Orkney and Shetland, and from there to the Sudreys, Scotland, Ireland and western England. They also make the long and dangerous voyages over the Western Ocean to the Viking settlements in the Faeroe Islands and Iceland. The

There is no more magnificent sight than a drakkar under sail. The embodiment of wealth and power, they are the Viking world's ultimate status symbol, the preserve of jarls and kings alone.

A byrding, the everyday coastal trader. This is the type of ship a wealthy farmer would use to take his produce to market – it's worth chasing one if you're short of provisions.

BELOW A knarr, a rugged and seaworthy long-distance trade ship. There's a good chance of finding something valuable in one of these: silk from Mikligard, furs from Gardariki, or walrus ivory from the White Sea, who knows?

OPPOSITE A snekke under sail. Fast, manoeuvrable, and drawing only 18 inches of water fully loaded, these small warships are ideal for a bit of opportunistic strandhogg by small raiding parties. Hit and run!

TOP The Viking round shield gives good protection to the body but leaves the head and lower legs exposed. One of these warriors is about to have his hamstrings cut – once he's on the ground he's done for.

ABOVE Use your shield to conceal a second weapon and give your opponent a nasty surprise.   RIGHT A warrior using the pommel of his sword to pull down his opponent's shield and leave his body exposed to a follow-through blow.

ABOVE This blow from a broad axe will test the swordsman's shield.

BELOW This spearman is in trouble. The swordsman has deflected the spearman's thrust with his shield and is now past the spearpoint and can simply hack it off, leaving him defenceless.

LEFT The two types of Viking battleaxe: the single-handed hand axe (left), and the two-handed broad-axe (right). The haft of the broad axe is twice the length of the hand axe's.

OPPOSITE ABOVE A disadvantage of the broad axe is that you can't use a shield at the same time. You're not completely exposed, however, because you can use the haft like this warrior to parry sword- and axe-blows.

Axes are not just for hacking. You can use the 'beard' as a hook to pull away an opponent's shield (left), or snag his ankles and pull him off balance (below).

The Frankish-style iron helmet with a nose guard is what most Vikings prefer to wear these days, if they can afford one.

BELOW The long sleeves of this mail-shirt protect most of the arms, while the shirt is long enough to protect the thighs too. Fastening a belt over it helps transfer some of the shirt's weight from the shoulders to the hips.

ABOVE Don't forget to pack a good leather water bottle. No man fights better for being thirsty.

voyage from Norway to Iceland takes about three weeks, almost all the time out of the sight of land. Unless you actually live in Iceland there is no good reason for a warrior to make this risky trip.

Useful navigation lore and sailing directions are passed down orally from generation to generation. If you want to become a navigator, you must become expert at reading sea and weather conditions, and the movement of wildlife:

- The Pole Star always points due north and the Sun is due south at midday.

- Keep an eye on the Sun: its height at midday will help you estimate your latitude (higher = further south; lower = further north), which is useful if you know the latitude of your destination.

- Though the height of the Pole Star can also be used in the same way to judge latitude, it won't help you much in the northern seas in summer because it's invisible in the night-long twilight.

- A build-up of cloud on the horizon may indicate the presence of land.

A Norwegian karve, a versatile craft suitable for raiding, trading or for a chief who just wants to travel to the annual thing in style with all his family and retainers.

- Know your seabirds: they can hint at the direction and proximity of land. During the breeding season (April till August – much the same as the sailing season) seabirds feed at sea, but return regularly to land to feed their young and to roost at night. Different birds range further to feed than others. Kittiwakes travel over 100 miles from land to feed. Smaller seabirds such as puffins and guillemots rarely travel more than six miles. Observing the flight of seabirds in the morning and evening gives reliable indications of the direction of land.

- Whales have regular migration routes and feeding grounds. These can help you locate yourself in the open sea. For instance, there is a regular whale feeding ground roughly halfway between the Faeroe Islands and Greenland.

- If the sea suddenly slackens in a storm it may be a sign that your ship has sailed into the lee of an island hidden by rain, fog or darkness.

- At night or in poor visibility, an experienced seafarer can sense how close he is to a coast from the strength of waves reflected from the shore onto the hull of his ship.

- The colour and clarity of the sea can provide further clues about your ship's position. Rivers wash silt into the sea, sometimes clouding it for miles offshore.

Sails *vs* oars

All Viking warships can be sailed or rowed. The usual square sails work best when the wind is blowing directly from astern. A Viking ship can make progress against the wind by tacking, that is by sailing a zig-zag course that repeatedly crosses the wind. This is always slow, hard work for the crew and puts a great strain on rigging and the hull. For this reason, a skipper usually waits until the wind is blowing in just the right direction before setting sail. This often leads to frustrating delays of weeks or even months. Patience is a virtue. A good chance to learn some skaldic verse.

In theory, a longship should not need a favourable wind, because it can be rowed. But try rowing into the wind for a few hours, and you'll understand why no major sea crossing is ever made under oars: it is desperately slow and exhausting for the crew. Oars are used mainly:

- for manoeuvring into and out of harbour;
- in confined and sheltered waters, such as fjords, when there is no wind or the wind is not blowing in the right direction;
- when sailing on rivers;
- when stealth is required: a ship's sail is often lowered to make it less conspicuous;
- for manoeuvring in battle: masts and sails are always lowered before battle to clear the decks for fighting.

Tip The hands of most men who work on the land will already be hard enough to row for long periods without blistering. If you are lucky enough not to work with your hands, practise rowing before embarking on an expedition. It will save a lot of suffering later on.

Portage

Sometimes you'll have to help haul your ship a short distance overland to avoid an obstacle, to get from one river to another or to avoid a long sail around a dangerous headland. Portages are most often necessary in Gardariki where rivers are the main highways. Ships are dragged overland at several places to pass from one river to another, while ships going south from Koenugard to the Black Sea also face many portages to avoid the wild Dnepr rapids. Portages are also used to bypass man-made obstacles such as fortified bridges, as the Danes did in 886 when the Parisians refused to allow them passage along the Seine.

*After first unloading any cargo, Rus merchants drag their boat
overland to avoid unnavigable rapids.*

Portages are hard work and, in hostile territory, dangerous too. The
ship must be unloaded and all its cargo carried separately. This is not
just to make the ship lighter to drag: without the buoyancy of water
to support it, a ship's keel may break under the weight of the cargo.
Logs are placed under the ship's keel to act as rollers, making it much
easier to drag. There is no guarantee of finding oxen or horses nearby
so ships must carry enough crew to drag them.

You and your companions will be very vulnerable to surprise attack
during a portage. The Dnepr rapids are notorious for this as Pecheneg
horsemen often lie in ambush for Rus merchants. In hostile territory,
always reconnoitre, post guards and keep your weapons handy.

Seasons for seafaring

If the signs are that the weather is settled, short sea crossings lasting no
more than a day and a night may be made safely at any time of year.
Even those who are most experienced in weather lore cannot accurately predict what is going to happen much further ahead than that,
so long voyages are rarely undertaken between late October and early
April when periods of settled weather are rare. Seafaring is dangerous
enough at the best of times; sailing in winter is just not worth the risk.

Ships are hauled out of the water around the end of October, and
the mast, sail and rigging are taken down and stowed away for the

winter. In Norway, ships are stored in long sheds, but elsewhere you'll see them just left out in the weather or placed in nausts, ship-shaped depressions with low sheltering earth banks on either side. The time to begin getting ships ready for sea again is the spring equinox, so that they can set sail as soon as settled weather returns. Plan to complete return journeys before the beginning of October when the winds will be regaining their strength. If you can't do this, and if it's safe to do so, spend the winter where you are and come home in the spring.

Surviving storms and shipwreck

In the evening one day, as darkness came on, it blew a gale. Before they were aware, breakers were both seaward and ahead. There was nothing for it, but to make for land, and this they did…. All the men were saved, and most of the cargo, but as for the ship, that was broken to pieces.

EGIL'S SAGA

No one loves the sea, it is a killer. Shipwreck is an occupational hazard of seafaring. Apart from foundering on the open sea, in which case you'll disappear without trace, the worst thing that can happen is that your ship gets blown onto a lee shore during a storm.

Skippers do not try to fight the elements if caught out at sea by bad weather. If the sea is not too high, the skipper shortens sail and simply allows the ship to drift before the wind. Only the most experienced seamen can manage the sails in a storm, but everyone else will be kept busy bailing for their lives. It's time to get seriously worried if you see the crew running ropes under the keel and lashing them tight around the hull: this is a desperate attempt to stop the ship breaking apart.

The great danger of drifting before a storm is of being driven onto a lee shore and wrecked. The skipper can give his crew the best chance of survival by hoisting full sail and steering straight for the land. The slightest error of judgment in the surf and the ship may broach-to, that is be overtaken by the waves and founder stern first, or slew broadside on to the waves and be capsized. Though the ship itself may be wrecked, and the cargo lost, it often happens that it gets close enough to land first for the crew to make it ashore safely.

Under these circumstances, the nature of the shore has a great bearing on your chances of survival. Shipwreck on a rocky shore is the worst. The waves may pound the ship into kindling wood against the rocks and batter you to death before you have a chance either to drown or scramble ashore. Depending on the strength of the waves, there is a better chance of surviving a shipwreck on a sloping sandy shore. In less violent storms the ship may simply be beached and can be re-floated at the next high tide, if …

… the locals don't find it first. Ancient custom, recognized almost everywhere, considers anything, and anyone, cast up by the waves to be the property of the finders. If your ship has beached, you'll probably still have your weapons, so you can keep the thieving locals at bay until the tide comes in. Bedraggled, unarmed survivors who have fought their way through the surf from a foundered ship are at their mercy, however. If this happens to you, being robbed of your jewelry and enslaved is the best you can hope for. If you're suspected of being a pirate and, let's face it, that wrecked longship washed up on the beach is pretty incriminating, you'll most likely be executed on the spot.

> Tip Learn to swim. Good swimmers are respected and you'll be able to enter swimming competitions, which even kings take part in. It might also save your life.

Preventing shipwrecks

> *Sea runes you must cut if you want to have guaranteed*
> *the sail-horses on the sea;*
> *on the prow they must be cut and on the rudder,*
> *and burnt into the oar with fire;*
> *however steep the breakers or dark the waves,*
> *yet you'll come safe from the sea.*
> THE LAY OF SIGRDRIFA

Mighty Thor, Odin's son, is the best protection against shipwrecks. Wear a Thor's hammer charm around your neck at all times when at sea. Even Vikings who have become Christians do this. Pray also to the sea god Njord who protects sailors.

Carving protective runes on the ship and on its oars can also prevent shipwrecks. Runes must only be carved by an expert. If you don't know what you're doing, they will be impotent or even harmful.

Many shipwrecks are caused by malevolent spirits stirring up the weather or sea currents. A fierce-looking figurehead helps scare them off. Always remove figureheads when approaching a friendly shore so as not to scare or offend the native spirits. Witches and wizards have the power to whip up storms or calm the seas. Keep them on your side!

LEFT *Shipwreck preventers: Thor's hammer charms are the best insurance you can get against being lost at sea.*

BELOW *Keep malevolent spirits away from your ship by mounting a suitably fierce-looking figurehead on the prow. Make sure it can be easily removed when approaching a friendly shore so as not to make enemies of the local spirits.*

Wind for sale

Finnish wizards offer wind for sale to sea-farers who are becalmed or kept in port by adverse winds. In return for payment, the wizards will give you three magic knots tied in a strap. Untying one knot provides a moderate breeze. Untying another brings a stiff wind, but untying all three at once brings an uncontrollable gale and your ship will likely be wrecked so be careful.

– 6 –
Have Longship, Will Travel

*Let the tillers of the soil of this land feel that we have
busied ourselves in their territory.*

HASTEIN (ACCORDING TO DUDO OF ST QUENTIN)

× | × | × | × | × | × | × | × | ×

R ight, you've got the gear and you know how to use it, you've joined
a raiding party, and the longship is rigged and ready to sail. The
world is yours to plunder: where are you going to start? The answer
depends on where you happen to live. Norwegians tend to head west
to Scotland, Ireland and the northwest of England. The Danes go
southwest to England and Frankia, or south across the Eastern Sea to
Wendland. The Swedes generally head east to Finland and Gardariki
(Russia). It's all down to geographical convenience really, but there is
nothing to stop a Swede joining a raid in the west or Norwegians and
Danes going to Gardariki.

Read on to learn what opportunities await you in the main raiding
destinations and what kind of reception to expect from the locals.
Forewarned is forearmed.

*A small raiding party approaches a defended shore. That's not the ideal
landfall – sail away and try somewhere else.*

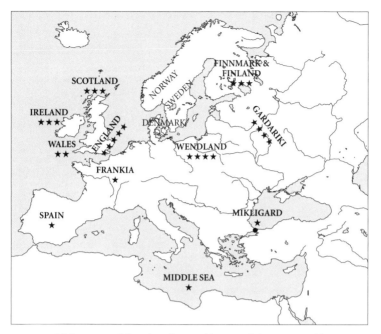

Make a note of these locations and how good they are to raid.

Raiding near to home

Just because you're a Viking, there is no reason to pass up an opportunity to plunder your fellow Vikings. It's generally forgotten now that we Scandinavians were busy raiding one another for centuries before we began to give the rest of Europe the benefit of our attentions. Unfortunately, because Scandinavians are now so used to piracy, there are few easy pickings left. You'll still have chances to snatch untended sheep and cattle when passing through the Danish and Norwegian islands, but most coastal settlements were abandoned long ago as their inhabitants moved to safer inland sites.

Many of the shallow fjords and inlets around the Danish and Swedish coasts that once gave easy access to inland areas are now obstructed with barriers of wooden stakes driven into the seabed. Breaking these barriers is not technically difficult, but the task wastes time, robbing the would-be raider of any chance of surprise. Trading

97

Barriers of wooden stakes like these are all too commonly found blocking the approaches to Danish and Swedish harbours these days. Clearing a path through would only take a few hours, but that's all the enemy needs to get organized.

places such as Birka in Sweden and Hedeby in Denmark are far from the open sea and are strongly fortified. And stake barriers protect their harbours from surprise seaborne attacks.

Further afield, the Viking colonies in the Faeroes and Iceland are not wealthy enough to justify the risks of the long open sea voyages needed to reach them. Nor do they offer good prospects for settlement anymore, all the good land having been claimed a long time ago. A few years ago, Erik the Red discovered a new land even further west, which he has called Greenland. Being uninhabited, there is certainly nothing there to interest a warrior.

Another problem is that kings these days are more powerful than they used to be and they get seriously annoyed if anyone other than themselves plunders their subjects of their wealth. There is little a free-lance Viking can do to protect himself from royal vengeance, so don't plunder the territory of your own king. The fact that kings also don't like their subjects raiding neighbouring kingdoms in peacetime adds another level of complication. There's even talk of the Danish kings introducing licences to raid! If you want to plunder in Scandinavia, it's best to do it as part of a royal army during one of the many wars our quarrelsome kings have with one another.

FINNMARK AND FINLAND

Rating ★★★

The Finns have always travelled by gliding swiftly on smooth boards...
As soon as they have done damage to their enemy, they shoot away in
the same lightning fashion as they flew to the scene. The nimbleness
of their bodies and skis combined gives them a practised ease
in attacking and retreating.

SAXO GRAMMATICUS, *HISTORY OF THE DANES*

Location North, where the sun never sets in summer and never rises in winter.

Inhabitants Ski-Finns (who call themselves Sami) and Finns.

Key resources Poor in treasure but rich in furs and other valuable commodities.

Finnmark is inhabited by the Ski-Finns, so named because they were the first people to travel over the snow on skis in winter. Ski-Finns have no permanent homes but move often, following the herds of reindeer, which they hunt for their meat and skins. The Ski-Finns' main wealth is in furs. They spend the winters hunting and trapping bear, fox, otter, reindeer and squirrel, whose grey winter fur, called minniver, is very precious. In summer they collect down from the nests of eider ducks, hunt seals for their hides and walrus for their ivory teeth and their hides, which we use to make ships' ropes.

East of the land of the Swedes, across the northern arm of the Eastern Sea, is Finland. The Finns who live here are farmers but, like the Ski-Finns, their main wealth is in furs. If you're single, you'll be interested to know that there are supposed to be many women among the Finns who desire sex with men, but do not want to marry. When these women have children, their daughters are very beautiful, but be warned: their sons are deformed, with heads in the middle of their bodies.

How hard to raid?

The Norwegians and Swedes raid the Ski-Finns and Finns to exact tribute in furs, especially the prized minniver. These they sell at great profit to the Franks, English, Greeks and many others. Neither the Ski-Finns nor the Finns are a match for Vikings in open battle, but they know it and rarely let us exploit our advantage. The Finns are well armed with iron spears and swords, but they prefer to avoid Viking raiders by hiding in the forests or taking refuge in stone forts, which they build on inaccessible crags.

Although the Ski-Finns lack the skill of metalworking and have few iron weapons, they are expert archers and make dangerous enemies. They use a distinctive recurved bow made by gluing together strips of wood with different characteristics: these have much greater power than Viking bows. They say that a boy becomes a man when he is strong enough to string one of these bows. Their arrows are tipped only with bone points, but they travel with such force that they can easily penetrate mail. The Ski-Finns prefer never to come to close quarters; instead they harry their enemies from a distance. They are

Steer clear of the Ski-Finns in winter. While you flounder, they glide over the snow on skis, picking their enemies off with arrows.

especially deadly in winter. Travelling on skis they can move faster than a flying bird, launching sudden attacks and then retreating quickly out of range.

Vast swarms of biting midges and mosquitoes make campaigning in the north unpleasant in the summer even if there is no resistance from the locals. Another danger of the Ski-Finns and Finns comes from their witches and shamans, who can conjure storms and fogs from nowhere. Their shamans defeated even the great Ragnar Lodbrok by sending a raging storm followed by furnace-like heat, which robbed his warriors of their health.

ENGLAND

Rating ★★★★

Archbishop Sigeric advised [King Aethelred] that money should repel those whom the sword could not: thus a payment of ten thousand pounds satisfied the avarice of the Vikings. This was an infamous precedent ... as soon as their old strength was recruited with rest, they returned to their old practices.

WILLIAM OF MALMESBURY, *DEEDS OF THE ENGLISH KINGS*

Location Southwest across the North Sea.

Inhabitants The English are mostly descended from Angles and Saxons, with some Jutes thrown into the mix.

Key resources Abundant livestock and portable goods as well as the odd thousand pounds from the generous King Aethelred.

Rich, green and fertile, England is *the* destination for the ambitious Viking at the present time. Since 978 England has been ruled by a foolish and unpopular king, Aethelred.

Aethelred came to the throne in suspicious circumstances, after his elder half-brother Edward was murdered by courtiers of his step-mother Aelfgyth. Who knows if Aethelred was a party to the murder – he was only ten at the time (but kings must grow up quickly) – but he has never been able to rid himself of the taint of suspicion and has struggled to win the loyalty of his people. Aethelred's unwillingness to listen to his counsellors has not helped his reputation.

For a long time, England was off limits to Viking raids, thanks to a succession of strong kings. Scenting Aethelred's weakness, Vikings began trying their luck again soon after his accession. After Olaf Tryggvason killed his ealdorman Byrhtnoth in a great battle at Maldon earlier this year, Aethelred paid him off with tribute of 10,000 pounds of silver rather than risk another defeat. Alas for the English, this has made the weakness of their king only too obvious to the Vikings and many more will soon be crossing the North Sea in the hopes of being paid off with similar munificence. To get your share, join the armies of one of the big beasts like Olaf, Thorkell the Tall or Denmark's King Svein Forkbeard.

A silver penny of England's cowardly king Aethelred. You'll be seeing plenty of these circulating round the markets, taverns and brothels of Scandinavia as homecoming warriors enjoy the rewards of their victories.

Nowhere in England is far from the sea and several broad estuaries – the Thames, the Wash and the Humber in the east, the Severn and the Mersey in the west – provide easily navigable routes far inland. The Romans once ruled Britain and they left behind a network of good straight roads. Many of these are still in good condition and mounted armies can travel quickly along them. Fast travel is also possible on the 'ridgeways' that run along the crests of the well-drained chalk hills of southern England.

England was the first country to be attacked by Viking raiders, almost exactly 200 years ago. The English (or Angles and Saxons as they called themselves then) were very familiar with Scandinavians as merchants and they were shocked when Vikings began plundering their trading places and monasteries. At that time England was divided into rival kingdoms, which did not cooperate against the Vikings. In 865, a great Danish army arrived under Halfdan and his brothers (see chapter 4) and quickly conquered half the country. Only Alfred's kingdom of Wessex held out.

While the Danes were settling on their conquered lands, Alfred reorganized his kingdom's defences. When Vikings again invaded Wessex in the 890s they found themselves thwarted at every turn. Even the wily Hastein got nowhere fast. Alfred's sons and grandsons were all great warriors too. They conquered the Danish settlements and the greatest of them, Athelstan, brought all England under his control and made it a single kingdom. Erik Bloodaxe was the last Viking leader to rule an independent kingdom in England. He came to a bad end in 954 (see chapter 3).

How hard to raid?

The English are not battle-shy and with good reason. Historically, they have won more battles against Vikings than they have lost and England's present weakness is entirely due to its poor leadership. Under Aethelred's predecessors, England was a strong military kingdom, more than capable of seeing off the largest Viking armies that came against it. Under a wiser king, expect England to recover quickly. All the more reason to get in there now.

It's easy for a Viking to feel at home in England. The English are not unlike ourselves. Their ancestors, the Angles, Saxons and Jutes, came from Denmark and Germany and they don't have much difficulty understanding our language. They've had such long contact with Vikings that they've even adopted many of our words. Although they are devout Christians, the English share our warrior values and enjoy the same style of bloodthirsty poetry.

Most important, the English fight on foot, like us, in a shield wall, with the same weapons we use. Like our armies, too, English armies are built around the warrior retinues of powerful landed men, the thegns (local chiefs like *hersar*) and ealdormen (regional lords like jarls), who owe military service to the king. The thegns and ealdormen raise the local levies of freemen who make up the greater part of the English army and lead them in battle. Like Byrhtnoth's boys at Maldon, the household warriors will fight to the death for their lords, rather than be dishonoured, but the levies are unreliable. If they have confidence in their leaders they will stand their ground. However, if they are badly led they usually run away when the fighting gets hot.

England is well provided with strongholds. Fortified towns called *burhs* have been built all over the country. These restrict the mobility of raiding armies by controlling the crossing places of major rivers and providing secure bases for local troops to gather. *Burhs* also act as refuges for the country folk in wartime. England's wealthiest city, London, on the Thames river, is secure behind rebuilt Roman walls. A bridge here is a formidable obstacle to any fleet trying to force a passage upriver to raid the rich lands beyond.

The English possess a large fleet, which is based at Sandwich in Kent. However, the fleet is not permanently manned and it takes weeks to gather crews for a campaign. English warships are similar to Viking longships and like them they cannot remain at sea for very long. For these reasons you don't need to worry much about being intercepted at sea before landing in England.

Once you are ashore, though, news of your arrival will spread fast: beacons set up on prominent hills quickly alert the whole countryside to danger, so you won't have the benefit of surprise for long.

IRELAND

Rating ★★★

You must be more afraid of [Irish] wile than [Irish] war; their friendship than their fire; their honey than their hemlock; their shrewdness than their soldiery; their betrayals than their battle line; their specious friendship than their enmity despised.

GERALD OF WALES, *THE HISTORY AND TOPOGRAPHY OF IRELAND*

Location The large island west of Britain on the edge of the Western Ocean.

Inhabitants The native Irish are divided into many tribes and kingdoms.

Key resources The usual story, but especially good for potential slaves.

Ireland is a deceptive land that appears at first sight to be quite weak, but which is, in reality, actually quite strong. Few places in Ireland can have escaped a visit by Vikings in the last 200 years, and many, especially their monasteries, have been sacked repeatedly. Thousands of Irish folk have been captured and herded to the slave markets. Ask a few slaves where they're from and you'll soon meet an Irishman.

Yet Irish resistance has never crumbled and all Viking attempts at conquest have achieved is the foundation of a few towns around the coast. These remain independent only because they are strongly fortified and, because they are by the sea, cannot easily be starved into submission by siege. Ireland has many navigable rivers, chief among them the Shannon, which provide easy routes inland, but travel overland can be difficult because there are a great many bogs and few roads. The Irish measure their wealth primarily in cattle, but, from a Viking's point of view, the country's main wealth is its people.

How hard to raid?

When Vikings first raided Ireland in the 790s it was divided into hundreds of small sub-kingdoms that owed a loose allegiance to a smaller number of high kings. Warfare between the kingdoms was constant and even Irish monks waged war with rival monasteries. These divisions made it easy for Viking armies to raid wherever they liked without much fear of meeting a large Irish army. Encouraged by their success, Norwegian Vikings founded raiding bases around the Irish coast in the 840s and tried to conquer territory for settlement. A few of these bases – Dublin, Wexford, Waterford and Limerick – are now prosperous trading towns, but the Irish quickly destroyed most of them.

Mobility is what makes Vikings successful and, by settling down, the Norwegians made themselves vulnerable to Irish counterattack. Another problem was that it's impossible to negotiate lasting peace treaties, as Vikings were able to do in England and Frankia. There are too many kings to negotiate with and what one of them agrees is never recognized by the others. Nor does defeating and killing a king in battle bring any advantage. The extended Irish royal families yield a never-ending supply of kings: no matter how fast you kill them, there's always another. Ireland's most powerful king today is Brian Boru, the High King of Munster. A fine war leader, he hammered the Limerick Vikings in 977 and may achieve greater things yet.

Most Irish sub-kingdoms can raise armies of around 300 men. This doesn't sound very impressive, but there are a lot of them. Sub-kings owe military service to their high kings, so a high king who can enforce the obedience of his vassals, like Brian Boru, can raise a very large army. Man for man, however, an Irish warrior is no match for a well-equipped Viking. The Irish fight almost naked without armour or helmets, using only bucklers (small round shields) for protection. Spears are the main weapons. The bow is rarely used, but they're mean shots with the sling and they also use a barbed javelin with a feathered shaft, which they throw very accurately. Recently, Irish smiths have begun making copies of Viking weapons. Because Ireland lacks iron, these are always smaller and lighter than the real thing.

ABOVE *A typical barefoot Irish warrior armed only with a spear and buckler. They'll really give you the run-around in those Irish bogs.*

OPPOSITE *A depressingly familiar sight for any Viking who has gone raiding in Ireland: a monastic round tower. If they have any warning of an attack, the monks take refuge in these with their valuables. You know you could take them if you had time, but you don't...*

The Irish won't willingly offer themselves up to your superior weapons. As far as possible, they avoid open battle. Instead, they'll let you chase them for weeks through bogs and pouring rain, harassing you with sudden ambushes, until, exhausted and frustrated, you give up and go home. It's not glorious but it works.

Ireland is well provided with fortifications, great and small. Just about every king has his stout stone round fort and there are literally thousands of ringforts designed to protect individual families. Ringforts have a circular rampart, with a palisade, and contain a single roundhouse and farm buildings. The ramparts are more effective at keeping livestock in than keeping Vikings out, but breaking in is the easy part. Under the floor of the main house is an entrance to an underground passage that acts as a refuge for the family and their valuables. Watch out: a few of these lead to secret exits outside the fort, but most do not.

You'd think winkling the Irish out of their holes would be easy, but it's not. Internal doors and hidden ventilation shafts make it difficult to smoke people out. The passages twist and turn so you can't sit at the entrance and shoot arrows down them hoping to hit someone. The low, narrow passages are easy to defend and quickly get blocked up with bodies if there is a fight underground. You could always dig the Irish out if you had time, but the trouble is that on a raid, you don't. Settle for taking the livestock and move on. Most monasteries these days have tall, round towers, with entrances high up the side that can only be reached by ladder. These are another

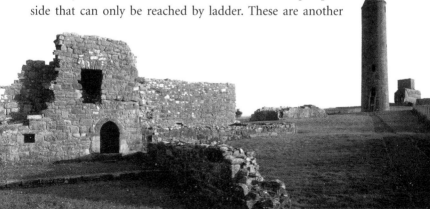

time-waster. Monks use these as refuges for themselves and their monastery's treasures. They can't hold out in their towers for long but they know that Vikings can't afford to get bogged down in a siege either.

Having no business sense, the Irish never take prisoners. An Irish warrior would much rather take your head home with him as a trophy than ransom you for any amount of silver. Irish warriors consider a good collection of severed enemy heads to be a status symbol, Vikings prefer silver. Be very careful when negotiating with the Irish: they have a reputation for using offers of peace talks as cover for ambushes and murders. The Viking Thorgils, whom the Irish called Turgeis, came close to conquering Ireland in 844, but he was captured and drowned by an Irish king using that kind of trick.

SCOTLAND

Rating ★★★

The hungry battle-birds were filled
In Skye with blood of foemen killed…
And many an island girl's wail
Was heard as through the isles we sail.

BJORN CRIPPLEHAND IN *THE SAGA OF KING MAGNUS BAREFOOT*

Location Head west across the North Sea.
Inhabitants Originally Picts, the Scots (from Ireland) have taken over.
Key resources Good grazing land if you can take it.

Scotland is that part of Britain north of the narrow isthmus that separates the Firth of Clyde in the west from the Firth of Forth in the east. It is an extremely mountainous land and the west coast is indented by fjords. Norwegians will feel at home there. At the time Viking raiding began 200 years ago, the country was known as Pictland, after its inhabitants, the Picts. The Scots, who are an Irish people, then ruled only the west-coast district of Argyll and some offshore islands. The rich Scottish monastery of St Columba on Iona has often been raided by Vikings, most recently by Danes in 986.

You won't have to face these Pictish warriors, with their distinctive square shields, if you invade Scotland today. They were conquered by the Scots over a hundred years ago and have since disappeared.

Norwegian Vikings conquered and settled the Orkney and Shetland Islands and the Sudreys between about 825 and 850. Sigurd the Stout, the earl of Orkney, now rules all these islands, as well as Caithness and Sutherland. Forced out of their west coast districts by Viking raids, the Scots pushed east and, under their king Kenneth MacAlpin, they conquered the Picts in 843. The Picts have not been heard of for a long time now and the Scots tell some strange stories about them, that they were blue, for example, or were dwarves who lived underground.

How hard to raid?

The Scots are more willing to give battle than other Irish. They have already dumped the Picts on the dung-heap of history, and have recently captured the English town of Edinburgh and made the Welsh of Strathclyde their vassals, so you'd be a fool to underestimate them. The Scots' military organization is based loosely on the English system: the core of the army is provided by the king's household warriors. The rest of the army is provided by the regional jarls, who in turn rely on local lords to raise levies from the districts they control. Like the rest of the Irish, they have adopted Viking-style weapons and are particularly fond of the two-handed war axe. Small forts are very common: many of them are built on artificial islands in lakes for extra security.

WALES

Rating ★★

The Welsh people are light and agile. They are fierce rather than strong, and totally dedicated to the practice of arms. Not only the leaders but the entire nation are trained in war.

GERALD OF WALES, *THE DESCRIPTION OF WALES*

Location A mountainous land bordering England in the west.
Inhabitants The Welsh, who also call themselves Britons.
Key resources Rich pickings from monasteries are your best bet.

Wales has only recently become a major target for Viking raids. This sudden popularity has nothing really to do with the attractions of Wales itself – it is not a rich land – but because raiding in Ireland has become more difficult. Fortunately, what wealth there is in Wales is concentrated in the more fertile coastal parts. The large and fertile island of Anglesey is the most prosperous and well-populated part of Wales and it is easy to raid because it is so near to Dublin and the Viking settlements in the Isle of Man. Four years ago Guthfrith Haraldsson of Man carried away 2,000 captives from the island. The interior of Wales is mountainous and poor and not worth the trouble of raiding.

Because it has not been raided as frequently as other countries, Wales still has monasteries near to the coast. The most important, the church of St David at Menevia in the south, was sacked in 967 and 988, but it has already recovered and is ripe to be plundered again. If you're looking for a quick return, Maredudd, king of Deheubarth, pays a silver penny a head to ransom any of his people who are captured by Vikings. For a bishop, the Welsh will pay 40 pounds of silver.

The Welsh are divided into half-a-dozen kingdoms. They are often at war with one another or with the English. At present, Maredudd's kingdom is dominant. Welsh kings often recruit Viking mercenaries into their armies. Maredudd is recruiting right now for a campaign against the neighbouring kingdom of Morgannwg.

How hard to raid?

The Welsh are extremely skilled at using their country's difficult terrain to their advantage, being experts at mounting ambushes. In battle, their favoured tactic is rapid attack, followed by rapid retreat, repeated again and again. You can never, therefore, assume that if the Welsh are running away, it is because they are beaten. There are many small forts in the country, most of them sited on inaccessible crags that make them very difficult to attack.

Kings keep a permanent retinue of household warriors, but all freemen are duty-bound to fight. Though they have little armour, Welsh warriors are strong and nimble: they train by lifting iron bars, wrestling and racing each other up mountains. The Welsh warriors most to be feared are their archers, who use a short, broad bow that is very powerful for its size. They can shoot accurately while running, whether in attack or retreat. Never regard a wound received at the hands of the Welsh as minor, no matter how superficial it seems: they are reputed to apply poison to arrowheads and spear points.

FRANKIA

Rating ★

A mounted Frank is irresistible; he would bore his way through the walls of Babylon; but when he dismounts he becomes anyone's plaything.

ANNA COMNENA, *THE ALEXIAD*

Location South through the North Sea and the narrow seas.
Inhabitants Franks, plus 'Normans' in the north.
Key resources You name it, it's there.

Once prime pillaging country, Frankia today is effectively off-limits for Viking raiders. Ironically, this is partly due to the success of earlier Vikings. Vikings first raided Frankia when Charlemagne was emperor, but he quickly saw where the trouble lay. Broad navigable rivers, like the Rhine, Seine, Loire and Garonne, are effectively high roads into the heart of the kingdom, with many towns and rich abbeys along them. Charlemagne kept the raiders out by building forts and stationing fleets and coastguards at their mouths. There was nothing that even a great warrior like him could do to protect the open coast, however. When King Godfred raided Frisia in 810 he was back home in Denmark with 200 pounds of silver before Charlemagne's army arrived on the scene.

When Charlemagne's grandsons started squabbling about their inheritances in the 830s, the Frankish coast defences broke down. Viking fleets sailed up the undefended rivers and plundered where they liked. Often, there was little opposition. The Frankish kings were more concerned with fighting their dynastic rivals than the Vikings, who they began paying off with tribute.

The Frankish kings also granted Viking leaders lands on condition that they agreed to keep other Vikings out. Hrolf, the leader of the Seine Vikings, was the most successful of these leaders. In 911 King Charles the Simple appointed Hrolf Count of Normandy. Hrolf's successors have kept their side of the bargain, turning Normandy into a no-go area for Viking raiders. The counts still welcome Viking mercenaries but it's not clear for how much longer: most 'Normans' now fight in the Frankish style, on horseback.

Charlemagne (r. 768–814) made the Frankish empire the greatest in Europe since the Romans. A great warrior, he had the measure of the Vikings, but his successors have not been of the same quality.

Normandy remains a safe haven for Vikings forced to flee England or just in need of a bit of rest and recuperation over the winter.

By the time the last of Charlemagne's descendants, Louis the Lazy, died in 987 (he was too lazy even to have any children), the Frankish monarchy had become weak and powerless. The new king, Hugh Capet, controls only a small area around Paris and his barons only obey him if it suits them. Don't be fooled into thinking that this makes Frankia weak. The barons, like Hrolf's grandson Count Richard, run their principalities efficiently and defend them well with castles and armoured cavalry.

How hard to raid?

It is Frankia's combination of cavalry and castles that makes Viking raiding a dangerous proposition anywhere other than along the open coast. An encounter with Frankish cavalry is something you won't forget in a hurry: they're formidable. The typical Frankish cavalryman is well armoured. He wears a long mail coat that covers the thighs as well as the body and arms, and a conical iron helmet with a simple but effective noseguard. For protection he also carries the long kite-shaped shield, which is specially designed for fighting on horseback.

The preferred weapons of Frankish cavalry are the javelin and the sword, but they also use maces (deadly against iron helmets), single-handed axes, and single-bladed fighting knives called falchions, which are like long seaxes. The cavalry fight in tightly packed formations of about 50 horsemen. Each has its own standard the horsemen follow in a charge, or rally to in an emergency. Their usual tactic in battle is to charge the enemy headlong and hurl their javelins before drawing their swords. Standing up to these charges takes great courage and discipline (see chapter 8). Frankish cavalrymen train for war by staging mock battles. Although weapons are blunted, they fight these battles with the same ferocity as real ones and deaths are not uncommon. Frankish cavalry are exceptionally glory-hungry and actively seek out single combats with opponents of equal status.

Frankish cavalry from Charlemagne's time.
Today they wear conical helmets with
noseguards and use kite-shaped shields
designed specially for fighting on horseback.

Because of the high cost of armour, weapons and horses, most Frankish cavalrymen are dependent upon a lord who provides their equipment and grants them a small estate for their upkeep in return for their service. Most Frankish foot soldiers are poorly equipped peasant levies who rarely stand their ground in battle. Frankish cavalry have complete contempt for the levies and, in their civil wars, kill them for sport.

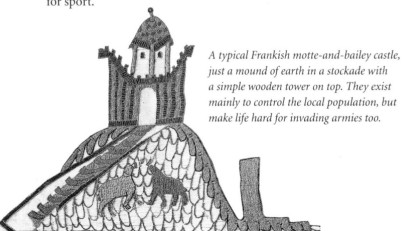

A typical Frankish motte-and-bailey castle,
just a mound of earth in a stockade with
a simple wooden tower on top. They exist
mainly to control the local population, but
make life hard for invading armies too.

Frankia is heavily fortified. Every city is walled and the countryside is thickly scattered with hundreds of small earth-and-timber motte-and-bailey castles and a smaller number of strong square stone castles. The stone castles are the homes of the great barons and they can withstand sieges of months or even years. The barons build motte-and-bailey castles in strategic positions to defend their lands from invaders. These castles consist of a wooden tower built on top of a natural or man-made mound (the motte) surrounded by a moated stockade (the bailey), which contains housing for the garrison and stables for its horses. Motte-and-bailey castles can't withstand a long siege, but that's not the point. Any delay is bad for a raiding force, especially when you know that a big cavalry army may be being gathered against you. But you can't safely ignore them either because their cavalry garrisons can ride out and harass you as you march, preventing foraging and picking off stragglers. So, Vikings steer clear of Frankia these days.

WENDLAND

Rating ★★★★

When the [Wends] knew of [the Danes'] coming they gathered together and began to resist manfully and to defend their property. Having obtained the victory [the Wends] massacred half the Danes and plundered their ships, obtaining from them gold and silver and much spoil.

RIMBERT, *THE LIFE OF ST ANSKAR*

Location South across the Eastern Sea.
Inhabitants Slavs called Wends.
Key resources Portable luxuries, notably silver, amber and slaves.

Wendland lies along the whole southern coast of the Eastern Sea. The Wends are divided into many tribes, including the Adodrites, Rugians and Pomeranians. They control the mouths of rivers, such as the Oder and the Vistula, that are busy trade routes to central Europe and the

Greek empire. As a result of this, the Wends possess many prosperous trading towns and have plenty of silver. The Wends also control the most important sources of amber.

How hard to raid?

Raiding the Wends is risky, but the rewards, in silver and slaves, make it well worthwhile. There's also the convenience factor. The Wends can be raided without making a long sea voyage so you can set out in early summer and still be home for harvest. Ideal for Viking family men.

The Wendish towns are well known to Scandinavian merchants, who visit them often to trade, so good intelligence is easy to obtain. None of the towns is situated on the open coast. Most are sited a few miles inland on rivers and inlets, so there is little chance of a raiding fleet approaching unobserved. All are well fortified with earth ramparts, timber palisades and towers. Arkona, the chief town of the Rugians, is sited on a high headland, with cliffs facing the sea and a rampart to landward. Jumne is garrisoned by the famous Jomsvikings who do not welcome other Vikings trying to muscle in on their patch.

The Wends are a warlike people: they even dress the idols of their gods in helmets and mail. Wendish warriors fight both on foot and on horseback. Foot soldiers fight with a large round shield and short spears, and usually wear little armour. They are extremely skilled at setting ambushes for the unwary. Be especially careful when pursuing fleeing Wends: they may be drawing you into a trap.

Wendish cavalry ride small, nimble horses. They attack by charging towards the enemy, throwing their spears and wheeling away quickly. Anyone who has fought the Franks will know that a spear thrown by a galloping horseman can very easily pierce shields and mail. The Wends build ships in the Viking manner and in recent years have launched their own pirate raids on Denmark, Sweden and even Norway. Because their ships and weapons look so much like ours, you can easily mistake them for Vikings. A sure way to tell the difference is to look at their heads: Wends crop their hair very close to the scalp.

GARDARIKI

Rating ★★★★

*Harald and jarl Rognvald got ships and went east that summer to
Gardariki to King Jaroslav and stayed with him all the following
winter.... Harald stayed three years in Gardariki and travelled widely
in the eastern lands. Then he set out for Greece, with a great following
of men, and he went to Mikligard.*

SNORRI STURLUSON, *KING HARALD'S SAGA*

Location East across the Eastern Sea.

Inhabitants Rus.

Key resources Slaves and furs, but the Rus are our friends so no
  raiding please.

Gardariki, the kingdom of the Rus, is where you'll find the Viking
partnership of commerce and violence at its most organized. You can
expect a friendly reception in Gardariki whether you've come to trade,
serve as a mercenary in its king's *druzhina* (warrior retinue), find a safe
place of exile or just break the long journey to Mikligard to join the
Varangian Guard. The kingdom gets its name from its many fortified
cities, the chief of which – Aldeigjuborg, Holmgard and Koenugard –
are all prosperous trading centres.

The Rus welcome Vikings, whom they call Varangians, because
they are themselves descended from Vikings. Back in the late 8th
century, enterprising Swedes noticed that high-quality silver coins
were finding their way to Scandinavia from somewhere on the other
side of the Eastern Sea. To find the source of the coins, they began
to explore the great rivers that flow into the Eastern Sea, founding
fortified towns as they went, or conquering native Finnish or Slav settlements. Sometimes dragging their boats overland to pass from one
river system to another, they found their way to the city of Bulgar on
the Volga river. There they met Saracen merchants from Baghdad in
Serkland, which turned out to be the source of the coins, as well as

other luxuries like silk and spices. They also discovered the Dnepr River, which flows into the Black Sea and gives access to the rich Greek city of Mikligard.

The Rus didn't have much of their own to trade so they used their towns as bases for raiding the neighbouring Slavs and Finns for tribute in slaves, furs, honey and beeswax, which the Saracens and Greeks are keen to buy. Sometime around 860, Rurik united the Rus into a single kingdom: his descendants rule it still. Since that time the Rus have intermarried with their Slav subjects. They still fight in the Viking way, on foot in a shield wall, but they now speak the Slavs' language and worship their gods. Three years ago Greek missionaries converted the Rus king Vladimir to Christianity. As is the way with Christians, now that he has converted, Vladimir expects all his subjects to do so too.

The Rus go on their tribute-gathering expeditions every November, when the first frosts harden the ground after the autumn rains. Trading expeditions start in the spring when the river levels are highest, making

The wealthy Rus city of Holmgard where, legend has it, Rurik founded his first kingdom. Easily reached from the Eastern Sea, this is the major centre for the fur trade and the jumping-off point to follow the rivers south to Koenugard and Mikligard.

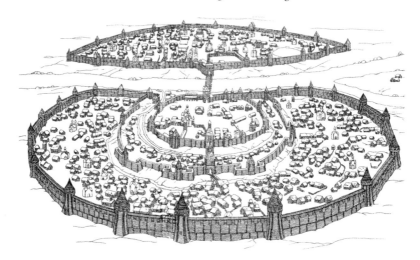

The baptism of the Rus king Vladimir in 988 by Christian priests from Mikligard was bad news for pagans. Now he expects all his subjects to become Christians too.

it easier to navigate shoals and rapids. The Rus usually trade with the Saracen merchants at Bulgar; a few have travelled all the way to Baghdad, sailing down the Volga and crossing the Khazar Sea to reach Serkland. They complete their journey travelling across mountains and deserts in caravans of camels (large, ugly, hump-backed animals that can carry heavy loads and seldom need to drink). The trade with the Saracens is less profitable than it used to be because their silver mines are becoming exhausted. As a result, fewer and fewer Rus go this way every year.

To trade with the Greeks at Mikligard, the Rus first sail down the Dnepr from Koenugard to the Black Sea. This is the most dangerous part of the journey. At several places it is necessary to drag ships overland to avoid dangerous rapids. Pecheneg nomads often lie in wait at these places to ambush Rus fleets. Battles are very common so the Rus are always in need of good warriors. On reaching the Black Sea, the Rus sail west and south along the coast to Mikligard. They return by the same route. Trade treaties with the Greeks forbid the plundering of merchant ships in the Black Sea.

Is it worth joining the Rus?

If you join the king's *druzhina*, it's certainly possible to make a good life for yourself in Gardariki and share the tribute from the Slavs, but terms and conditions are not as attractive as those in the Greek emperor's new Varangian Guard (see chapter 2). If you're after the big money (and milder winters), carry on to Mikligard.

MIKLIGARD

Rating ★

Tófa and Hemingr had this stone raised after their son Gunnarr,
but he died out in Greece. God and Mother of God help his soul.

11TH CENTURY RUNIC MEMORIAL STONE, NORRSUNDA, SWEDEN

Location Across the far side of Gardariki on the southwest shore of the Black Sea where it joins the Middle Sea.

Inhabitants Mostly Greeks, though as capital of their empire, you'll find all sorts there.

Key resources Don't raid here – get paid as a Varangian instead!

Capital of the Greek empire, mighty Mikligard is probably the largest and richest city in the world. If this inspires you to plan on raiding the place, a word of advice – don't. Mikligard's riches are well guarded and those who try to seize them by force face a literally hot reception. On the plus side, the city offers excellent opportunities for trading plunder and captives obtained elsewhere, and for well-paid mercenary service in emperor Basil's Varangian Guard (see chapter 2 for terms and conditions).

Mikligard is known to the Greeks as Constantinople, after the Roman emperor Constantine, who founded the city nearly 600 years ago. Constantine couldn't have picked a better place. Mikligard stands on the Bosphorus, a narrow strait that separates Europe from Asia and links the Black Sea to the Middle Sea. Being at this natural crossroads quickly made Mikligard into a great and wealthy trading place, visited

Mikligard (the 'great city') didn't get its name for nothing: it is the largest, most magnificent and richest city in the world. There is no better place for the ambitious Viking warrior to make his fortune as a mercenary.

by merchants from all over the world. Its harbours are always crowded with merchant ships and its warehouses are filled with wine, oil and grain, and the precious silk cloth from Serkland. In the city there are many palaces, monasteries and vast churches, all of them filled with gold and silver treasures as well as the mouldering body parts of the Christian holy men called saints, which the Greeks believe have magic powers to cure diseases.

How hard to raid?

When you see the Greeks of Mikligard, with their long silk robes and watered-down wine, you'll think they couldn't start a fight in a tavern never mind rule a great empire. Being fabulously rich helps: they can afford the best mercenaries from the four corners of the world. Also, these effete city-dwellers aren't typical Greeks. Just as well they're not responsible for defending the city. Most Greek soldiers are recruited in Asia Minor on the other side of the Bosphorus. It's a high, mountainous land, freezing cold in winter and blistering hot in summer, and it breeds hard men.

Even more important, if you're thinking of making a pass at it, Mikligard has the world's mightiest fortifications. It's in a natural defensive position, on a peninsula, with the Bosphorus on one side and on the other a long sheltered harbour called the Golden Horn. In wartime an iron chain is stretched across its entrance to keep hostile ships out. Both land and sea approaches are protected by massive stone walls with stout towers topped by powerful catapults. The land walls are awesome; there are three lines of them to get through. The weapon that can breach them hasn't been invented yet.

Thanks to its strong defences, Mikligard only needs a small garrison. The rest of the Greek army is on the frontiers. Foot soldiers and cavalry have about equal importance in the Greek army, and they're both well armed and armoured. Greek soldiers wear unusual coats of scale armour that looks like the skin of a giant serpent. This is made of iron plates fastened together with leather cords. The foot soldiers fight in formations much like our shield wall. Their job in battle is to pin down the enemy formation while the cavalry outflanks and surrounds it. If you're ever in combat against a Greek shield wall, make sure someone is watching your back. The Greek heavy cavalry called cataphracts are an impressive sight. They're protected from head to toe with mail and scale armour so that only their eyes are visible. Even their horses wear coats of scale armour, so they cannot be easily brought down by arrows or spears. They're not fast, but with all that weight of iron, they're hard to stop once they get going.

In 941, the Rus Vikings Got a Hot Reception: Greek Fire

The emperor Romanos called the ship carpenters into his presence and said to them: 'Make haste and get the old galleys ready for service without delay. Moreover, put the fire-throwers not only in the bows but at the stern and both sides as well. When the galleys had been equipped according to his instructions, he collected his most skilful sailors and bade them give king Igor battle.... The merciful and compassionate Lord willed not only to protect his worshippers who pray to him and beg his aid, but also to give them the honour of victory. Therefore God lulled the waves; for otherwise the Greeks would have had great difficulty hurling their fire. As their galleys lay surrounded by the enemy, the Greeks began to fling their fire all around: and the Rus seeing the flames threw themselves in haste from the ships, preferring to be drowned in the water than burned alive in the fire. Some sank to the bottom under the weight of their armour: some caught fire as they swam among the waves; not a man escaped that day save those who managed to reach the shore. For the Rus ships by reason of their small size can move in very shallow water where the Greek galleys because of their greater draught cannot pass.

LIUDPRAND OF CREMONA, *THE EMBASSY TO CONSTANTINOPLE*

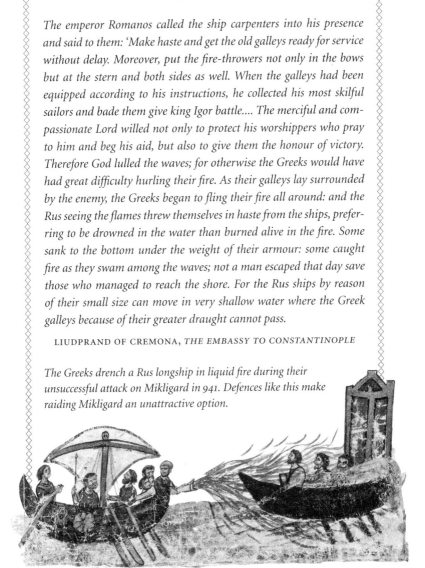

The Greeks drench a Rus longship in liquid fire during their unsuccessful attack on Mikligard in 941. Defences like this make raiding Mikligard an unattractive option.

123

The Greek army is the least of a Viking's problems: the Greek fleet is the strongest in the world. Greek warships are called *dromons* and they are more than a match in battle for any longship. Like longships, *dromons* are driven by both sails and oars. They have two masts, each carrying a triangular sail. This shape of sail allows a ship to get much closer to the wind than a Viking square sail does. The smallest *dromons* have 100 oarsmen, 50 to a side sitting in two banks one above the other. The really big ones have 200 oarsmen arranged in a similar way. In addition, *dromons* can carry up to 100 soldiers. Wooden towers mounted in front of the masts support powerful catapults.

Worse still, at their bows the *dromons* carry fearsome machines that snort like bellows and spew liquid fire. The formula of this 'Greek Fire' is a closely guarded secret. It can burn a ship and its crew in moments and is so hot that it even sets the sea itself on fire. There is no defence against Greek Fire: burn with your ship or jump over the side and drown, it all depends on whether you prefer to die hot or wet. The Viking fleet that attacked Mikligard in 941 was completely destroyed by this weapon. To escape, head for shallow water where the deeper-draughted *dromons* cannot follow.

Beware also the devious diplomacy by which the Greek emperors incite their enemies to fight one another. The Rus king Svyatoslav was killed in this way 20 years ago. While he was raiding Greek lands, the emperor arranged for the Pecheneg nomads to ambush him when he was returning home.

SPAIN and the MIDDLE SEA

Rating ★

The Northmen sailed up the Garonne as far as Toulouse, wreaking destruction everywhere, without meeting any opposition.... Some of them ... got to the southwestern part of Spain, where they fought long and bitterly with the Saracens, but were finally beaten and withdrew to their ships.

ANNALS OF ST-BERTIN, C. 844

Mail-clad Moorish archer and cavalryman. Moorish soldiers are full-time professionals and make formidable adversaries.

Location Spain lies far south of England, beyond Frankia. It guards the entrance to the Middle Sea, which is otherwise reached by overland travel across Gardariki.

Inhabitants Dark-skinned Moors in the south, fairer-skinned Christians in the north.

Key resources Food and drink, plenty of treasure.

Well done if you get this far! Spain is dominated by the Moors, a dark-skinned people who also rule North Africa. The Moors follow the Muslim religion and are often at war with the Christian kingdoms that rule the north of the country. Córdoba, the Moors' capital city, is almost as large and rich as Mikligard and Spain has many other wealthy cities, especially in the south. The climate is warm and sunny. Wheat, oil and wine are plentiful. What's not to like?

Plenty. Spain's wealth has often tempted Viking raiders, but more often than not they have suffered heavy losses at the hands of the Moors. What can be said about the wealth of Spain can be said of the lands around the Middle Sea many times over. However, Vikings have only once raided the Middle Sea. That was in 859–62 and despite being led by the greatest of all Viking leaders, Hastein (see chapter 3), they lost two-thirds of their ships. The safest way to profit in these lands is to sell slaves as the Moors are always eager to purchase fair-skinned boys and girls.

How hard to raid?

The Moors have a large and well-organized professional standing army of foot-soldiers and light cavalry. This enables them to react quickly to any threat. The spear and the bow are the main weapons of the foot soldiers, while the cavalry rely on the javelin. Royal armouries make 20,000 arrows every month so expect to come out of any engagement with the Moors looking like a hedgehog. Both infantry and cavalry also use light straight swords and wear mail or scale armour and iron helmets. The Moors' finest warriors are the mamluks. They are slaves, usually bought as children and brought up as warriors, but unlike our slaves they are respected and can become wealthy and influential. The Moors protect their cities with stone walls and towers, the tops of which support stone-throwing machines, and there are many strongly garrisoned castles along the coasts to deter pirates.

It is difficult for Vikings to enter the Middle Sea in part because of the powerful Moorish fleet and in part because of geography. To enter the Middle Sea from the Western Ocean, all ships must pass through the narrows of Narvesund, which are only nine miles wide. This makes it almost impossible for a raiding fleet to get through undetected and unchallenged by the Moors' own fleet of galleys. These are like Greek *dromons* and they have always proved superior to Viking longships in battle. Fortunately, the Moors do not know the secret of Greek Fire. If a raiding fleet ever does get through to the Middle Sea again it will have rich pickings, but it will still have to get out again, past an enemy who will be alert and waiting – and, like as not, eager for revenge!

Life on Campaign

He who means to take another's life or property should get up early.

HÁVAMÁL

× | × | × | × | × | × | × | × | × | × | ×

C ampaigning isn't all about battles and looting. It isn't even mostly about battles and looting. You'll spend far more time sitting in camp talking about battles and looting than actually doing either. Or you'll be on the road getting rained on, getting sore feet from marching or, if you're lucky, a sore backside from riding. And getting hungry. It's easy to tell the difference between a rookie Viking and a veteran. A rookie breaks into a house and looks for treasure. A veteran breaks in and looks for the food store. Only if the army is secure, comfortable and, above all, fed can it fight and plunder effectively.

Planning

Good intelligence is essential in planning a campaign. Take into account the political situation in the area. Exiles, former high-rank hostages and merchants are all good sources of this sort of information. Political

A warrior probably filled some idle moments in camp carving this stirring scene of a large Viking fleet drawn up on an enemy shore.

difficulties, such as disputed successions, and civil wars deserve to be exploited. Christians can often be taken by surprise if attacked during religious festivals. In 842, Norwegian Vikings captured Nantes almost unopposed because the whole town was celebrating the Christian festival of Saint John the Baptist and no one was on guard.

Find a friendly merchant: they will have up-to-date knowledge of the most prosperous trading centres, their defences and the routes of access to them. Merchants will also know about the success or failure of the most recent harvest. Avoid areas that are in the grip of famine as it will be impossible to live off the land. It was famine, rather than enemy resistance, that brought an end to the last great Viking campaign in Frankia in 892.

Do not fail to seek advice from the gods. This is usually done by casting lots. Take a branch from a fruit-bearing tree and break it up into small sticks. Mark these with cuts and scatter them on a spread-out sheet. A priest should then pick up three sticks at random and, depending on the marks he finds on them, answer yes or no to questions you ask him. If the omens are bad, plans should certainly be changed, as the gods do not like to be defied by mere humans. A Danish army planning to seize and plunder the Swedish trading centre

One-eyed Odin (left), hammer-wielding Thor (centre) and fertility god Freyr (right). Never fail to seek the advice of the gods while on campaign. Odin, especially, is wise and has much to teach.

at Birka in around 851 changed its plans after a soothsayer cast lots and announced that the gods were against it. When the Danes asked where they should go instead, they were told to plunder a city in Wendland. The Wends were unprepared for the attack and the Danes returned home with ships full of plunder, proving the wisdom of taking omens seriously.

A *seiðr* woman (seeress) is able to foretell the future by consulting with spirits. These she draws near to her through chanting and singing, having dined on a ritual meal of the hearts of many different animals. *Seiðr* magic is dangerous. *Seiðr* women can misuse their magic to kill, manipulate people's minds, steal and cause shipwrecks: always treat them with respect.

Pack a spade

> *The Danes were there, the most powerful people among the*
> *Northmen, who had never been heard to have been captured*
> *or conquered in any fortification.*
>
> ANNALS OF FULDA

It's not enough getting loot. When you've got it, you've got to keep it, as its former owners are likely to want to try to get it back. For this reason, building fortifications is an essential skill for a Viking.

When a raiding fleet first makes landfall, it anchors a safe distance offshore while scouting parties are sent ashore to check for the presence of hostile forces. The first thing that happens on landing on an enemy shore is making camp. Ships are a source of vulnerability once the army is ashore and they need to be protected. They can't just be left lying around on the shore. Ships are valuable, and if they can the enemy will steal them or, if they haven't the time or the manpower to do that, they'll burn them. Then you're stuck. During a strandhogg (see chapter 8) some men must always be detailed to guard the ships while others plunder. A larger force intent on campaigning for a season or more will always build a small fort to protect the ships, loot and stores, and to provide an emergency refuge for the army if the camp is attacked. Longships can't carry much in the way of stores, so organize foraging parties at once to search out provisions.

You may have to live in camp for several months, so pick a sheltered and well-drained place. A little way upstream on a sheltered river estuary is ideal, close enough to the open sea that you can reach it quickly if you need to leave in a hurry, not so close that an enemy fleet can fall upon you by surprise. Ideally, you should also consider the wider strategic position of the camp. In 892 Hastein built his fort on the banks of Milton Creek in north Kent. From there he could threaten the rich farmlands of Kent, sail west up the Thames, cross the estuary to East Anglia, or head east to Frankia if things went badly. Which they eventually did.

Fortifications don't need to be very elaborate. A simple U-shaped earth rampart, opening to the water, with a ditch in front and a timber palisade on top is quite enough to prevent a quick assault on the ships. Embedding sharpened branches on the rampart adds an extra difficulty for attackers. It is important to match the length of your ramparts with the number of men available to defend them. A formula used by the English reckons that one man is needed to defend every four feet of wall, that's about the same as you'd expect in a shield wall. If they haven't all fled, force the local peasants to do the digging for you. It won't take them long, if they know what's good for them. Islands in rivers are another good bet and they don't need fortifying either. Olaf based his army on Northey Island in the Blackwater estuary last summer and everything worked out pretty well for him.

If the army is likely to be based in the same place for more than a single season, as Viking armies in Ireland often were, it is worthwhile investing some more of the local peasants' time and effort in building some decent houses for the winter and in strengthening the camp's defences by facing the rampart with turf blocks or a timber revetment. Don't feel guilty about this (as if you would): their own lords don't treat them any better. No one respects peasants; that's why you became a Viking, remember? If you don't want to have to rebuild the defences

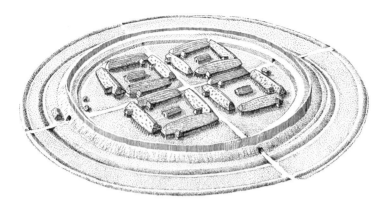

A Viking camp built by the Danish king Harald Bluetooth at Fyrkat in Jutland. Don't expect the camps you build while on campaign to be this neat and orderly.

after a couple of years, use fire to harden the points of any stakes that are to be driven into the ground. This will protect them from rot.

Deciding on an appropriate garrison to leave behind when the army sets off on its summer plundering expedition is tricky. There won't be many volunteers, either, because those who stay behind will miss out on the joy of raiding. Leave too many and it risks weakening the army in the field. Not enough and the enemy may be able to storm your camp and take your ships and any loot and prisoners you've left there. Even the best leaders can get this wrong. Hastein lost the lot, including his family, when Alfred's men took his camp in East Anglia in 893.

Under some circumstances it can be worthwhile abandoning your ships. The Danes who invaded in England in 865 weren't planning on going home and put all their effort into conquering territory. All is not lost, either, if an army does lose its ships. The Vikings who invaded Frankia in 891–92 abandoned their ships in Flanders, but just forced the Franks to provide them with new ones when they decided to move on to England.

Winter break

In the month of February 886 an army of eastern Franks was sent into
Gaul against the Northmen who were near Paris. However, when they
arrived there, the Northmen, who were well stocked with all things in
their fortifications, did not want to fight with them, nor did they dare to.

ANNALS OF FULDA

Campaigning usually stops in winter. The weather is bad, the roads
have turned to mud and there is no fresh grass to keep the horses
healthy. An army cannot survive a winter living in leaky tents or
makeshift shacks: cold, hunger and disease destroy armies just as effectively as defeat in battle. If you've not already gone home with your
loot, it's time to find comfortable winter quarters. Ideally, capture an
enemy stronghold or a town with ready-built houses and defences. If
defences are lacking, build them, as the Danes did at Nijmegen in 880
and Louvain in 891. An attack is unlikely because the enemy will also
usually demobilize for the winter, but don't be complacent. Guthrum
almost seized Wessex by attacking in January 878, when Alfred thought
the Danes were safely settled by their fires in winter quarters. Keep
your weapons and armour handy – and sharp – in case you need them
in a hurry.

After security and shelter, the most pressing problem for a raiding
army in winter is finding enough provisions. Men on campaign need
to eat well to remain effective. In practice this means that an army of
a thousand men needs to obtain about 2,000 pounds of bread, 1,000
pounds of meat and 240 gallons of beer (at least) every single day.

Small war bands and even large armies on the march can easily live
off the countryside they're passing through in summertime. Without
good management, any army that stays in the same place for six
months while it winters can very quickly use up all the local food supplies and begin to starve. This happened to Halfdan's men when they
wintered at Reading in 871. Viking foragers had to range wider and
wider, rejoicing over the discovery of a bag of seed corn in the same
way that the previous summer they would have celebrated finding a

sack full of silver. The West Saxons punished them for it mercilessly, sending bands of cavalry to roam the countryside and cut down the isolated foragers.

Some basic precautions:

- Don't take winter quarters in an area you've already ravaged earlier in the summer. If you did a proper job of it, there won't be much left to eat.

- Good intelligence is essential. By the time the landowners and the church have taken their rents and tithes, the local peasants won't have large stores of food for the winter. Identify and seize the places where the landowners and the church store their hefty unearned share of the harvest.

- Offer safe passage for merchants to come and trade with you. Hoisting a shield high on a pole and opening the camp gates is the traditional way to do this.

- As time passes, foraging parties will need to travel further and further from the safety of winter quarters to find supplies. Ensure that the parties are large enough to defend themselves if they do run into an enemy war band.

- Dispersing the army over the countryside makes provisioning easier but has obvious risks. You need to be very sure that the enemy can't launch a surprise attack if you're going to do this.

Tip (This one comes from Odin, from the *Hávamál*.) No man should take even one pace away from his weapons when on the march – you never know when you'll need your spear.

Odin with sword and spear

Horses

Not everywhere is easily accessible by ship. Though you won't have the risk of drowning, overland travel is much slower than travel by water, especially if you're forced to travel on foot. In wet weather you'll spend most of your time floundering in mud. Since speed is very much of the essence when it comes to successful Viking raiding, this just won't do. For anything other than a quick hit-and-run raid close to the sea, you're going to need horses.

It is possible to get a horse into a longship, but they don't make good sailors, they can't help with the rowing and they don't leave much room for anyone else. One of the Danish armies that moved from Frankia to England in 892 took its horses with it, but this was on the very short sea crossing from Boulogne to Kent, less than a day's sail away. Rather than take your own, it's much easier, and a lot cheaper, to acquire your horses when you arrive at your destination. The locals will usually be (fairly) happy to donate the horses you need without too much heavy-handed persuasion. They'll be hoping that you'll use the horses to ride off quickly and plunder someone else. You can always come back and finish the job later anyway. That's what Ivar and his Danes did when they invaded England in 865. After spending the

Landing horses on an enemy shore. Horses give an army essential mobility on land, but they're difficult to transport by ship for long distances. It's usually better to acquire them locally.

winter in East Anglia, they forced the East Angles to give them horses. The East Angles hoped they'd seen the last of them when the Danes rode off to attack Mercia and Northumbria. Some hope. Three years later, the Danes came back to stay.

Tip If you have a choice, don't pick a light-coloured horse: it will be too easily seen when you are riding in the dark.

It is crucial to remember that it is always easier to get in than get out. You'll be moving much more quickly when you set out on campaign than you will be when you're on the way back. If things go well, you'll be accumulating plunder all the time. Coins and silverware and the like can easily be put in sacks and packed on horses or carts, but some of your most valuable plunder will be captives. They'll be on foot and in no hurry at all to get to the slave markets. Some gentle encouragement may be needed to keep them moving and they'll need constantly guarding to make sure they don't try to escape. No doubt you'll also acquire some livestock for provisions.

By the end of a campaign, the whole countryside will be in a state of high alarm and, if you haven't already brought them to battle and defeated them, the enemy will have had plenty of time to gather their forces. Smoke rising from burning farms will show the enemy exactly where you are and, unless they're amazingly stupid, they will know exactly where you've left your ships or built your winter camp, so they'll also know where you're going. In other words, you'll have lost the advantages of mobility and tactical surprise that you had at the beginning, so you're now much more vulnerable. If confronted by a superior force, it is better to abandon your plunder and run than fight and lose: while the enemy is 'liberating' your plunder you'll have plenty of time to escape. There is always next year.

Tip Protect yourself against fatigue when on the march by putting mugwort (common wormwood) in your shoes. This helps ward off evil spirits and wild animals too.

Keeping dry

It is not good to get wet and cold. While the farmer can take refuge in his home, the warrior on campaign may have to spend days in the open, so take a good cloak. Sealskin is best, but very expensive. Greased leather cloaks are also very effective, but the seams need constant re-proofing if they are to keep water out. A cloak made from raw (i.e. unwashed and un-dyed) wool still contains natural oils that make it very water repellent, but it will become heavy in prolonged rain. Regular treatment with oil or grease keeps leather shoes water-repellent. Sealskin shoes and boots are the most waterproof.

Fashionable leather shoes made by the best Viking craftsmen. They may look great, but they won't keep your feet dry for long in wet weather.

Signalling

Horns are used for signalling at sea, on campaign and in battle. Learn to recognize the different calls for landing and putting to sea, for arming, for calling back parties of pillagers, for joining battle, and for advance and retreat.

Women

Women fight as warriors only in sagas, but no army can easily do without them – and that's not only because they keep a man warm at night. Many warriors take their wives and even their children on campaign with them, and many others acquire wives, concubines and slave girls along the way.

If women are ever a liability to an army, it is only because they must be protected. Women perform most of the domestic tasks that make camp life bearable – cooking and brewing; washing and repairing clothes; helping men bathe and dress; and caring for the sick and treating the injured – thus freeing the men to fight and forage, or just to sit around talking and drinking beer.

Women can also shame men into fighting harder – no man likes his woman to think he's a coward. When Vikings assaulting Paris in 885 fled from the walls, weeping and tearing their hair in despair because of the strength of the defence, the jeers of the women sent them back to try again.

Women: they may be gossiping as usual, but no Viking army can easily get along without a few in tow to cook, wash, sew and look after the sick. Some men take their wives, others acquire their women locally.

Personal hygiene

> *Combed and washed every man should be*
> *And fed in the morning;*
> *For one cannot foresee where one will be by evening.*
> REGINSMÁL

Vikings are proud of their reputation for being clean and well groomed. Being on campaign is no excuse for letting yourself go – don't let the English girls down, they find Vikings much more attractive than their own smelly, unwashed menfolk. Wash every morning if you can and bathe once a week, whether you need it or not. Don't waste heated water – let someone else use it when you've finished with it. Pack a fine bone comb and use it daily to keep your hair tidy and nit free. Get your clothes laundered regularly. If your wife didn't come along, find a substitute smartish.

Diseases spread rapidly through army camps, often claiming more men than battles. The worst killer is dysentery, also called the bloody flux. No one ever got into Valhalla by dying of radical diarrhoea, so, just in case your army doesn't have a healer, this is how to treat the illness. To begin with, give the patient colewort (wild cabbage) juice to drink and make him eat a broth of peas, vinegar and leeks, or a mixture of leeks, waybread (greater plantain), old cheese, goat's milk and goat's grease. If the patient begins to mend, give him roast cheese and dry bread to eat, and rosewater and sour wine to drink until he is fully recovered.

Nits can make the toughest warrior miserable so be sure to take a good comb with you on campaign.

Killing time

Camp life can be boring. Drinking, slave girls and conversation will be your staple entertainments – like they are at home. Keep in training for fighting by staging competitions for wrestling, sword-fighting, spear-throwing and archery. Any army led by a king or jarl is likely to have a skald along with it to entertain the warriors and compose verses praising the valour of his patrons. Balls for a rough-and-tumble game of *knattleitr* are easily made of wood or leather. Dice take up no space in a pack. A *hnefatafl* board can easily be scratched out on a wooden board or flat stone, while the counters can be made out of almost anything.

OPPOSITE ABOVE *A good quality* hnefatafl *board, but you can save space in your pack by simply scratching one out on a plank or flat stone if you need one.*

OPPOSITE BELOW *This unusually long piece of runic graffiti was left by Vikings exploring Greenland.*

Betting on dice games, board games, ball games, horse fights, drinking competitions and quite probably even two flies crawling up the prow of a longship, is always popular. Beware bad losers and cheats (with loaded dice, for example). Gambling disputes often turn violent and can destroy friendships. Many a warrior has come home empty-handed from a successful campaign because he didn't know when to stop gambling.

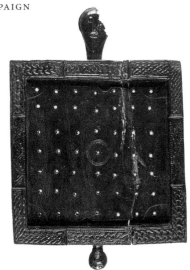

Security

Keeping valuables safe on campaign can be a problem. That's one of the reasons why arm rings were invented, so warriors could carry their wealth securely on their arms. Burying your loot in a hole in the ground is the safest option, but make sure it's near some distinguishing feature so you can find it again when you want to recover it. If your army is defeated, it may be several years before you'll get a chance to return for it. If you're killed, some lucky peasant years hence may find it instead.

Halfdan was here

Vikings are well travelled and those who know their futharks often like to inscribe their names in runes on a prominent landmark, such as a statue, or a pillar in a church, so that the people they've visited don't forget them (as if burning their towns and monasteries wouldn't be enough).

– 8 –

Battle

Be resolute in combat but never hot-headed.

THE KING'S MIRROR

× | × | × | × | × | × | × | × | × | ×

Make no mistake, battle is the surest route to glory. But only a madman or a berserker (often the same thing) should be in a hurry to go into battle, for the outcome is never certain. Always weigh the risks against the benefits first.

In the balance

Against:

- You might lose: historically, Vikings have lost as many battles as they have won. Defeat could ruin your plans for the summer raiding season and even see you drinking mead in Valhalla rather sooner than you might have liked.

- You might need to find a new *hirð*: even if he survives, a commander's reputation can be ruined by defeat so his warriors (those that are still alive) won't stay loyal for long.

For:

- You might win: historically, Vikings have won as many battles as they have lost. With the enemy's forces dead, demoralized or dispersed you can pillage at will and you will have won a strong hand for negotiating payments of tribute.

- You might get rich: victory makes a commander's reputation and delivers the means to reward his warriors. Warriors like a confident, competent and generous commander. One who refuses battle too often may get a reputation for faint-heartedness and lose his warriors.

- A chance to prove yourself: battle is the best arena for any warrior, from freeman up to king, to win personal glory for daring feats of arms. Glorious deeds get the young warrior noticed and build his reputation. Even in defeat or death, the warrior who fights heroically can still add to his reputation.

The balance of risk favours a Viking. For him, the benefits of victory outweigh the costs of defeat: for the defender, the costs of defeat outweigh the benefits of victory.

Full-scale battles are not common in Viking warfare. The warrior who goes a-viking for a few seasons simply to make enough to buy a farm and settle down may never take part in a real battle. Battles are uncommon because the price of defeat is very high, and it is especially high for our victims. The Franks, the English and other victims of Viking raids often seem downright cowardly in their reluctance to fight – and their willingness to buy off Viking armies. But try to look at it from their point of view. If they fight and lose, their whole country is left exposed to Viking pillaging and they'll have to pay tribute.

Battle scenes on one of those marvellous picture stones you'll see marking warriors' graves if you visit the big island of Gotland off the coast of Sweden. The scenes show battles from legends and the slain warriors' glorious welcome in Valhalla.

For our opponents, fighting also does not have the benefits that it has for the Viking raider. They are fighting in their own country so there is no opportunity for them to plunder to offset the costs and risks of a campaign. It is much better for the defenders to maintain an army than to risk everything on a battle. Just keeping an army in the field inhibits Viking activity, restricting their freedom of movement and their ability to plunder freely. The payoff from victory is much higher for a Viking army but, even so, much can be gained without fighting. A wise commander only seeks battle when he can be confident of winning.

Victory depends on good preparation

1 The commander must pick an advantageous battlefield and form his warriors up in the best formation. If he doesn't, then it's too late to do anything about it once the battle begins, because…

2 The commander must fight in the front ranks. Viking warriors expect this and it inspires them to fight as hard as him. The commander gains moral authority by sharing the same risks faced by his warriors, but the downside is that, surrounded by the shield-din and metal-storm of battle, it is impossible for him to control events once the first spears have been thrown.

3 Be prepared to fight on foot, whether you've marched or ridden to the battlefield. Even commanders do not fight on horseback – it would give them the means to escape in the event of defeat and allow them to abandon their foot soldiers to their fate. Every warrior would know this, so it would be bad for morale. Horses are sent to the rear. They must be guarded.

4 A good, brave, reliable man is needed for standard bearer. He won't have much chance to defend himself and he'll be a prime target for the enemy. Warriors take their directions in battle from the position

A standard bearer holds firm despite the carnage all around him. It takes a man of extraordinary steadiness and courage to be a good standard bearer because he must stand in the front ranks with his lord but is unable to defend himself properly.

of the standard, so if it goes down or is captured, confusion reigns. All warriors, and not just Vikings, see losing their standards to the enemy as shameful. They are equally jubilant to capture standards, knowing how demoralizing it is for their enemies, and it's one of the best ways to precipitate a general rout.

Tip If you're going into battle with Sigurd the Stout, the jarl of Orkney, and he asks you to be standard bearer, just say no. It's not an honour, it's a death sentence. Sigurd's famous raven banner was made for him by his mother, who is a sorceress. The banner guarantees victory to Sigurd, but death to the man who carries it. At a recent battle with the Scots, Sigurd lost three standard bearers before he was victorious.

Choosing a battlefield

The key thing about battles is choosing and exploiting obstacles.

Useful obstacles:

- ditch
- cliff
- rocks
- wood
- river

The side that gets to pick the battlefield can gain a strong initial advantage. An open battlefield is best, as it allows the commander to see what's going on and makes forming up easier. A commander who expects to fight a defensive battle should try to get the advantage of height or pick a position that has some **natural obstacle** in front of it. This need not be anything very big to be effective. A field ditch that a man could easily jump over takes on a whole new dimension when a couple of hundred men with spears are standing on the other side.

Most armies form up for battle in roughly linear formations. The larger army always has the advantage here because it can envelop the flanks of a smaller army without weakening its centre. A weaker army preparing for a defensive battle, or trying to deter an attack altogether, should try to anchor its flanks against a **difficult obstacle**, such as a river, cliff or dense wood. If no such obstacle is available, the commander of the weaker army is in a bind. If he matches the enemy shield wall in depth, he will likely be outflanked and surrounded, but if he stretches his shield wall so that it is as long as the enemy's, it will be thinner and more easily broken.

A commander who wants to bring on a full-scale battle must be careful not to pick a position that looks so completely unassailable that he may frighten the enemy off. The trick is to create a false impression of vulnerability. The skill is to pick – you guessed it – an **obstacle** that

OPPOSITE *Two armies form up in shield walls facing one another. Note how the warriors' shields are slightly overlapping, showing that they are in a good tight formation, ready for battle.*

looks like it can be crossed easily, but which will actually disorganize and break up an enemy formation. Marshy ground, a short steep
grassy slope that might go unnoticed from a distance, patches of rocks,
or a small, hidden, ditch could all fulfil this requirement.

But don't pick a position surrounded with obstacles! Remember
to consider escape routes in case things go badly. Try to avoid fighting
with a river or cliff at your back, for example. At the battle of the Dyle
in 891, the Franks trapped a Viking army against a riverbank: hundreds
of Vikings drowned trying to escape and two kings were killed and 16
standards lost.

Commanders like to give their warriors a stirring pep talk before
the battle starts, to fill them with fighting spirit by reminding them
of their grievances against the enemy and the spoils of victory, and to
make sure that everyone knows what is expected of them. He will pay
most attention to the less-experienced warriors, checking that they are
holding their shields and weapons correctly, that they know their place
in the battle line, and that they recognize pre-arranged trumpet calls
and the standards of their own leaders so that they know which direction to advance and where to rally in an emergency.

Fair play

If both sides are equally eager for combat it sometimes happens that
the rival commanders send envoys to agree and mark out a battlefield
in advance. They will try to choose an open and level site that offers no

obvious advantages to either side so that the outcome is decided solely by strength and skill at arms.

> *Messengers were sent to King Olaf from Athelstan challenging him to a pitched battle, with Vin Moor [Brunanburh 917] near Vin Forest as the battlefield.... The battle was to be fought in a week's time and whoever arrived first should wait up to one week for the other.... Some of his men Olaf sent up to the moor where the battle was to be fought, to choose camping sites and make things ready for the main body of troops. When they came to the place selected for the battle, the hazel rods were already set up [by Athelstan's men] and the battlefield itself fully marked out. The choice of ground had to be made with great care, for it had to be level and big enough to line up a great army. That is what had been done in this case: the battlefield was a flat moor with a river flowing on one side and a large wood on the other.*
>
> EGIL'S SAGA

Tip Avoid fighting in wet weather. Wet bow strings become slack and our smooth-soled leather shoes give next to no grip on wet grass or mud. No one can maintain the integrity of a shield wall in such conditions.

Make a good show

Establish a moral ascendancy before the battle starts by looking and sounding like winners.

- Dress as magnificently as you can manage. Clean and polish your weapons and armour the night before you expect to fight. Unfurl your standards and wave them triumphantly, as if you've already won. Commanders should wear bright, distinctive clothing so that they stand out in the battle line and their warriors can see them more easily.

Case Study

At Maldon last summer, both commanders were equally eager to fight, but both armies held effectively unassailable positions. Olaf's Viking army was camped on an island in a river estuary, which was linked to the mainland by a narrow causeway. Byrhtnoth's English army was formed up on the mainland opposite and held the mainland end of the causeway. When the Vikings attempted to cross to give battle they were easily held off by just three English warriors. It would have been just as easy for the Vikings to hold off the English if they tried to cross over to the island. Fearing that, if they could not be brought to battle, the Vikings would just take to their ships and sail off to raid somewhere else, Byrhtnoth deliberately gave up his position at the end of the causeway and fell back to allow the Vikings to cross. Byrhtnoth got his battle – but lost.

- Make a big noise. Shout as aggressively and loudly as you can manage and beat your shields with your weapons. Blow the war trumpets. Let the enemy know what you're going to do with their wives and daughters after the battle.

- Eat and drink before the battle if you get the opportunity. Your morale will flag if you're hungry and thirsty even before the fighting starts. But don't get drunk. It may make you feel braver, but it will impair your judgment: remember Odin's advice 'the more a man drinks, the less he knows'.

- Pray to your favoured gods for success: they may not listen, but it can't do any harm. Odin is the god of war, but he is mainly for the kings and berserkers. Thor, who defends gods and humans alike with his mighty hammer Mjöllnir, is the most reliable of the gods for the common man. Archers and those about to go into single combat pray to Ull, the archer god.

- Now is the time for the berserkers to work themselves up into their terrifying battle frenzy, biting their shields and howling. Make sure that the enemy can see and hear them. It's sure to unnerve them because the berserkers have such a ferocious reputation.

- The traditional Viking way to open a battle is to throw a spear right over the enemy army. This is to honour Odin, whose spear Gungnir stirs up warfare in the world and has the power to determine the outcome of battles.

What to expect

Every aspiring warrior wants to know what the experience of battle is really like. Any veteran will tell them that no amount of words can really prepare anyone for their first battle. If you survive, you'll truly understand why the warrior deserves more respect than other men.

Many old-timers say that it is the waiting before the battle begins that is worst. Berserkers may be able to work themselves up into a fearless battle frenzy, but most lesser mortals experience anxiety and fear, which they do their best to hide with as much bravado as they can muster. Remember that every man's fate is fixed and that there is no knowing when you will face the verdict of the Norns. Death will come at its appointed time whatever you do, so you might as well fight bravely and hope that it's not your day just yet.

On top of the fear of death or injury, if you're a combat virgin you will also be worried that you might not be as brave as you thought you were. Cowards face the worst sort of social disgrace, being declared a *niðing*, but it's not fear of disgrace or even courage that really keeps warriors in the battle line, it's the strong bonds of loyalty that develop between them. Few men can bring themselves to abandon their friends in such a difficult situation, even at risk to their own lives. In any case, no matter how much you might want to run away you won't be able to, if you find yourself in the front ranks of the shield wall, because of the press of men behind you.

A mail-clad king fights as he should in the front rank with his warriors (though most prefer to wear a helmet rather than a crown in battle). It is essential that a leader is seen to be taking exactly the same risks he is asking his warriors to take.

Fighting usually begins with an exchange of missiles as the two armies come within range. Both sides hope to disrupt the other side's formation before the close-quarters fighting begins. Men in the front ranks are most vulnerable to thrown spears. Arrows, falling on steep trajectories, can cause casualties anywhere. If you don't have a helmet your head will feel very exposed, but if you raise your shield to ward off falling arrows you expose your body to flying spears, which follow a shallower trajectory.

Once the shield walls clash, the hail of missiles dies down. If you're in the front rank you'll have the toughest time. Spears, swords and axes now come into their own, thrusting and hacking at bodies and shields. The noise is deafening. The press of bodies makes it hard to use weapons to best effect and, as long as everybody's shields hold together, casualties can be surprisingly light. Men in the second rank are within striking range of the enemy and can both give and receive spear thrusts, but those further back can play little part in the battle at this stage except lend their weight to shoring up the battle line. As men in the front ranks fall, warriors behind them move forward to fill their places in the shield wall.

[King Lyngvi] and his brothers went against Sigurd with a mighty force, and then the fiercest of battles began between them. Masses of spears and arrows could be seen flying through the air, axes swung violently, shields were split, armour was cut open, helmets were slashed, and skulls were cloven. Many men fell to the ground.

THE SAGA OF THE VOLSUNGS

Confusion is everywhere. Each man fights his own battle. You'll be aware of little except your comrades on either side of you and the enemy warriors immediately in front of you. You may have very little idea about how the wider battle is going. The best rule is to follow the commander's standard. If it is advancing, press forward mightily – the battle is going well. If the standard is being pushed back, give ground gradually to keep the shield wall intact.

It will be difficult for you to protect yourself and strike effectively at the enemy at the same time. To make a really good spear thrust or get a clear swing with a sword or axe, you'll have to expose much of the right hand side of your body. Just as you are doing the most damage you can to the enemy, you are also at your most vulnerable. Get over it, you can't win by trying to keep yourself safe.

As men tire and shields shatter, casualties begin to mount and the ground gets slippery with spilled blood and guts. You'll find yourself stumbling over dead and dying men – but keep on your feet! Falling is fatal. Lots of blows will be aimed at your unprotected feet and shins in the hopes of bringing you down. Even if you are not seriously hurt, getting up again can be difficult in the tightly pressed mass of warriors. There is a serious chance of being trampled to death by your own side even if an enemy spear doesn't finish you off. In a long fight, if you're lucky, a truce may be arranged so that men on both sides can treat their wounds and remove the injured from the battlefield.

You'll see disembowelled men screaming in agony, severed limbs and heads, and fountains of blood. Sword- and axe-strokes can almost literally cut a man in two lengthways, spilling brains and guts all over the place. This is the horrible reality of the skaldic songs but, thankfully, you won't have time to reflect on it until after the battle.

Individuals and small groups of warriors may succeed in forcing their way through the enemy shield wall. If they are not immediately supported, the enemy shield wall may re-form behind them and they will be cut off and surrounded by the warriors in the rear ranks. No matter how hard they fight it is only a matter of time before they are cut down. If a breakthrough can be reinforced and widened, it can spell the beginning of the end for the opposing shield wall. This is the point in a battle where many warriors begin to lose their nerve. Fearing that they are about to be cut off and surrounded they start to flee the battlefield. Those who still have the stomach for the fight should try to fight their way through the enemy ranks and rally to their commander's standard.

Tip Throw spare shields over wounded men to protect them from further injury.

When to run away

A good sign that a battle has begun to go badly is when the men in the shield wall start hunching together. When blows are raining in from all sides this is natural enough, but the sense of security this gives is illusory and it should be resisted. If the ranks become so tightly packed that the dead cannot fall and the living cannot wield their weapons effectively, defeat becomes almost inevitable.

If an army keeps its nerve and discipline, defeat need not turn into a rout. If the shield wall remains intact, an army can disengage in good order without suffering serious casualties, although it involves abandoning the dead and injured, and their war gear, to the enemy. In such circumstances, pursuit is unlikely. After a hard fight, the victors will be too exhausted to follow up their triumph and the defeated army can quickly regroup and continue its campaign if losses were not too great.

Indecisive outcomes are common. Back in 870 the Danes fought five battles against the West Saxons, winning three and losing two, without either side achieving a decisive result. The Danes withdrew, but were still strong enough to conquer Mercia, and come back a few years later to have another go at Wessex. Even after Alfred's famous victory over them at Ethandun in 878, Guthrum's Danes were still strong enough to negotiate a good peace deal.

Flight is the best option only if the shield wall has collapsed, but it's never a good one. If you flee you will expose your back to the enemy and you will not be able to protect yourself. Heavy casualties can be suffered during this stage of a battle, but pursuit does not usually continue for long. The victors are as tired as the vanquished and are usually more interested in plundering the dead than in killing for the sake of it. Your pursuers won't want to risk missing out and will soon turn back. They have possession of the battlefield and their exultant shouts of triumph will ring in your ears, but at least you'll still be alive.

Tip A good rule is, if in doubt rally to the standard. If you can't see the standard, you're really in trouble.

Facing a cavalry charge

At some point, you may have to fight an army (probably Frankish) with a cavalry division. Nasty, but effective. Here's what you should do if they come at you at full gallop.

- Keep your nerve and hold your ground
- Kill the horses
- Use natural or man-made obstacles to destroy the momentum of charging cavalry
- Take extra precautions against a flanking attack

It takes real courage for foot soldiers to stand their ground in the face of a full-on cavalry charge. A loose infantry formation caught in the open doesn't stand a chance, but a good shield wall can hold its own so long as everyone keeps their nerve. Horses instinctively shy away from obstacles, especially if they are bristling with sharp points. Their riders know this, but are hoping that their opponents don't and that they will break and run at the last moment. This is fatal. A horseman is ideally positioned to thrust a spear at the exposed backs of fleeing men and inflict deadly head wounds with a sword. They are also able to pursue you much further than foot soldiers can.

If the shield wall stands its ground, the cavalry will turn away at the last moment, hurling their javelins. These fly with much greater force than those thrown by foot soldiers and can easily penetrate shields and mail. Men will die, but as long as there are fresh warriors to step forward from the rear ranks and take their place, the shield wall cannot be ridden down. The horses are easier targets than their riders. Bring the horses down and their riders are easy meat.

If the enemy is known to have cavalry units, there are two ways you can prepare before battle is engaged. Protect your flanks by lining up against some natural obstacle. That way the cavalry won't be able

A well-disciplined shield wall stands firm against a cavalry charge while a warrior takes a swing at one of the horses, hoping to bring its rider down.

to use their speed and mobility to make a flanking attack, which can quickly throw a shield wall into disorder. Of course this means they'll come straight at you from the front, so destroy their momentum by digging pitfalls in front of a defensive position to bring the horses down and break their legs. Sharpened stakes driven into the ground in front of the shield wall are also very effective.

After the battle

Victory is a great opportunity to re-equip yourself at the expense of the slain. Move quickly: everyone else will have the same idea. Apart from weapons and armour, many of the slain will have been wearing jewelry and fine, if now blood-stained, clothes. Not all the bodies lying around on the battlefield will be quite dead. Minimize the chance of becoming a casualty of death-bed heroics by cutting their throats quickly and cleanly or giving them a smart crack on the head with an axe. If they were too badly injured to get themselves off the battlefield they are probably going to die soon anyway. Finishing them off quickly is really doing them a favour.

Stripping the slain after a battle is an opportunity not to be missed. Go for the most expensive items first, like mail shirts and swords.

Some of the defeated enemy may have surrendered, if they could not flee, in the hope of saving their lives. Bind prisoners well and guard them until you have decided what to do with them. There may be men of status whom you can ransom; able-bodied men can be sold as slaves. However, large numbers of prisoners can often be a burden to an army on the march, so it is often best to kill them.

If the skalds are to be believed, it was once the custom after a battle to honour Odin with a 'blood eagle' human sacrifice. This must have been something to see. The victim, usually a prisoner, had his ribcage cut open either side of his spine and, while still alive, his lungs were torn out to form the shape of an eagle's wings. The sons of Ragnar Lodbrok are said to have killed King Ella of Northumbria in this way in 867 to avenge their father whom the king had thrown into a pit of poisonous snakes. It was also once the custom to throw weapons into a river or bog as an offering to thank the gods for victory, but people do not have the same respect for the gods these days.

> **Tip** Do not volunteer to execute more than two prisoners. It is well known that if your face changes colour after killing three men, it is a certain sign that you will not long outlive your victims.

Small unit actions

While it's the big battles that the skalds sing of in the mead halls, skirmishing, plundering and burning by small bands of warriors are more typical of what you'll experience on most Viking expeditions.

Strandhogg This is the simplest kind of Viking raid, suitable even for a single ship's crew. The spirit of strandhogg is opportunism. Spot an untended cow or sheep grazing near the beach when you're sailing past: land, catch it, bundle it into the ship, and clear off as fast as possible. You'll be long gone before anyone notices. It's a case of spotting the chance of some easy plundering: a sleepy fishing village with no one on watch or a lone trade ship with a small crew, for example. If it's clear you've been spotted and there are armed men waiting, keep moving. No one can stay alert all the time, sooner or later you'll catch someone off guard.

> *Thirteen pirate ships set out from the land of the Northmen and tried to plunder the coast of Flanders, where they were repelled by*

coastguards. However, because of the carelessness of the defenders some dwellings were burned down and a small number of cattle were stolen. When the Northmen made similar attempts to raid at the mouth of the Seine, the coast guards attacked them and the pirates retreated empty handed, losing five men killed. Finally, on the coast of Aquitaine they met with success and thoroughly plundered the village of Bouin, returning home with immense booty.

ROYAL FRANKISH ANNALS

Hall burning Hall burning is common in bloodfeuds at home, but the techniques can just as usefully be applied to raids on farms and aristocratic residences abroad. If possible, reconnoitre the place secretly in daylight. The attack is best made during the early hours when everyone should be asleep. Station men outside all of the hall's entrances and if possible set some men all around the hall in case there are any secret ways out. Then set fire to the roof. The occupants will have no time to arm themselves properly before smoke and flames force them out of the hall. Emerging only one or two at a time through the doors, they can easily be cut down even if they considerably out-number the attacking force. Don't set fire to barns and outbuildings until you know what's inside them – they may contain valuable food stores and livestock.

A single archer defends his home and his wife against a raiding party. Once the attackers get round to setting fire to the roof, he'll be forced out into the open and they'll make short work of him.

Egil pushed the burning end of the log up under the eaves of the roof,
where the faggots soon began to burn. The people drinking inside the
hall had no idea what was happening until they saw flames pouring
from the ceiling. They made a rush for the door but it wasn't easy
going, partly because of the blazing timbers, partly because Egil was
at the door barring the way. He cut men down both in and outside the
doorway. In no time at all the hall was burned to the ground
and of all those inside not one survived.

EGIL'S SAGA

Sacking a monastery Surprise is the key to a successful raid on a monastery. If the monks have any warning, they will bury the monastery's treasures and even the most painful tortures will often fail to persuade them to reveal where they have been hidden because they believe that suffering for their god will secure them an honoured place in the afterlife. Monasteries often cover a large area. As well as the church there are the monks' dormitories, store houses, kitchens and workshops. The whole precinct may be surrounded by a wall. These are not defensive walls like those around fortresses and cities and they are easily scaled. Before launching the attack, send parties to cover all the routes out of the monastic precinct to prevent any monks escaping. Many monks are healthy well-fed young men who will fetch a good price at the slave market. Sustainability is the watchword when raiding monasteries, so no senseless burning just for the fun of it. If the buildings are left intact, monks will return and re-establish the community and, in time, it can be raided again.

The monks will offer little or no physical resistance, but they will freely call upon their god to wreak vengeance against those who dare to violate his holy places. There are plenty of stories attesting to the Christian god's powers and the dreadful punishments he has meted out to Viking raiders, such as the Viking whose bones shrivelled away after he had raided a monastery near Paris in the 840s. These are all probably invented by monks to frighten people; try not to let them get to you.

Raiders set fire to a town house. Sometimes, Vikings offer the locals a chance to save their houses by paying ransom. Looks like this lady didn't pay up.

Taking and sacking a town

Sacking towns is harder now than it used be. When our forefathers first started raiding overseas, towns were rarely fortified; now fortifications are the norm and you'll be lucky to take a town without a lengthy siege. Ports are often the easiest targets because, while they may have walls protecting them from attack by land, they often have an open waterfront so that goods can easily be moved between ships and store houses. The same principles apply to sacking a town as apply to sacking a monastery, though it takes a larger force to seal off all escape routes from a town. Skilful management of this part of a raid netted almost the entire population of Southampton in 980.

Townsfolk bury their valuables for safekeeping as a matter of course and if they escape, they will stay buried. Use whatever coercion is necessary to persuade captives to reveal any hidden hoards of coins or treasure (it's just tough luck if they really haven't got any – who is going to believe them?). As with monasteries, there is little point in wanton destruction and completely indiscriminate killing, glorious though it is. The sooner the town recovers from an attack, the sooner it can be hit again. The Frankish port of Dorestad on the Rhine got hit every year from 834 to 837 and still recovered. The town has long been abandoned but that's not our fault: the Rhine changed course and left it high and dry. The long-term survival of trade centres is in Vikings' interests in another way too: plunder and tribute provide us with most of our trade goods and they're not worth much if there is nowhere to sell them.

Sieges

Vikings are successful because they are masters of mobile warfare. Settle down anywhere for a long time and you start to become vulnerable to counterattack. The enemy has time to raise forces and knows exactly where to find you. For this reason, sieges are not recommended. Sometimes, just the threat of a siege can be enough to persuade townsfolk to agree to pay tribute – sieges are bad for business after all and that's the lifeblood of towns. So, it makes sense to try to negotiate and agree terms for surrender, offering, for example, to spare the lives and property of the inhabitants in return for a fixed payment of tribute. The besieged know what will happen if the city falls after it has refused terms. It is universally accepted by pagans, Christians and Muslims alike that no mercy need be shown to the garrisons and populations of fortresses and cities that have refused such an offer.

If the people of a fortified town won't be intimidated, the options are limited. People build walls around their towns for a good reason – they work. Sieges are rarely successful. If a fortified city can't be taken quickly by a surprise assault or by treachery (bribing someone to open a gate, for example), then it probably won't be taken. Remember that Paris held out for nearly a year against the Danes in 885–86 and was never taken. Usually, therefore, it is best to bypass a defended town, and keep moving.

The idea of a siege is to starve the inhabitants into submission. Trouble is, unless you have secure supply lines, it is usually you, the besiegers, who start to starve first. If the defenders have had any time at all to prepare, the grain stores and livestock of the surrounding countryside will have been moved to safety within the city walls. You will have to forage over wider and wider areas in search of provisions, making yourselves vulnerable to attack by enemy scouting parties. Life in a siege camp is unhealthy too and it is not long before men start to die of disease.

> **Tip** Never start a siege unless your army is large enough to cut off all supply routes to a fort or city. Even small amounts of food reaching the besieged population boosts their morale and strengthens their will and ability to resist. The longer a siege goes on, the longer the enemy has to raise a relief force.

But if all this isn't enough to put you off taking a city, build a fortified camp as you would in any other place where you are based for any length of time. The besieged will launch raids to try to destroy siege engines and cause casualties and general confusion. The danger is greatest at night. A fortified camp is also necessary for protection against attacks by enemy forces if any are active in the countryside (harassing foraging parties, for example) and as a refuge if attacked by a relief force.

Storming a fortified city is one of the most difficult and dangerous operations a warrior can be called upon to do. The defenders have most of the advantages during an assault (height and cover, and, often, heavier weapons) and if you do succeed in scaling the walls under a hail of arrows, spears, boulders, and boiling pitch you are really not going to be in the best of moods. No one can blame you if you take out your anger on the people whose intransigence (assuming they refused to surrender or negotiate) has forced you to endure such a terrible experience.

Successful assault of a fortress depends on the use of specialized siege weapons such as mangonels and ballistas, and siege towers for scaling walls. Viking armies don't carry these weapons with them. Carpenters and blacksmiths can make them on the spot in a matter of days if they are needed. Mangonels are powerful catapults used to throw rocks to batter walls. Ballistas are giant crossbows which are used as long-range anti-personnel weapons: they're ideal for keeping the defenders' heads down when an assault is in progress. They are

The Perils of Siege Warfare

The Lochlanns [i.e. Norwegian Vikings] did not abandon the siege [of Chester], for they were hardy and fierce, but they all said that they should make many hurdles, and that posts should be placed under them, and that they should perforate the wall under [the shelter of] them. This project was not deferred; the hurdles were made, and hosts were [placed] under them to pierce the wall, for they were covetous to take the city.

What the Saxons... did, was to throw down large rocks, by which they broke down the hurdles over their heads. What the others did to check this was to place large posts under the hurdles. What the Saxons did next, was to put all the beer and water of the town into the cauldrons of the town, to boil them, and spill them down upon those who were under the hurdles, so that their skins were peeled off. The remedy which the Lochlanns applied to this was to place hides outside on the hurdles. What the Saxons did next was, to throw down all the beehives in the town upon the besiegers, which prevented them from moving their hands or legs from the number of bees which stung them. They afterwards desisted and left the city.

ANNALS OF IRELAND

good defensive weapons for fortresses and are widely employed by the Franks and Greeks. Ballistas are very powerful. At the siege of Paris in 885–86, a single bolt from a Frankish ballista skewered seven Danes before losing its momentum. Both mangonels and ballistas get their power from torsion created by twisted ropes.

Tip When assaulting fortified bridges or city walls close to riverbanks or harbours, lash two ships together side-by-side to make a stable platform for a siege tower.

FIGHTING AT SEA

Piracy

> *On their way south towards Dublin [Svein and his raiding party] came*
> *across two merchant ships en route from England loaded with a very*
> *valuable cargo of English broadcloth. Svein made for the ships and*
> *challenged them, but they offered little resistance, and Svein and his*
> *men robbed them of every penny they had. The only things they*
> *left the English were the clothes they wore and some food, and*
> *after that they rowed away.*
>
> ORKNEYINGA SAGA

A merchant ship is a desirable prize that is likely to be filled with all manner of desirable goods. Merchant ships are slower under sail than longships and, as they are not built to be rowed, they have no chance of escape if there is no wind. Merchant ships have smaller crews than longships and are easily taken once they have been intercepted. If the crew put up any resistance, it is usual to kill them all unless there are any passengers – a bishop or a nobleman for example – who are worth a ransom. If there is no resistance, most Vikings content themselves with robbing the crew of their valuables and cargo and then set them free. For the best chance of catching a merchant ship, wait out of sight in small bays or inlets along the main trade routes to ambush them as they follow the coast.

Two longships lurk in a bay waiting to ambush a merchant ship. This might be how Vikings got their name: the word means 'men of the bays'.

Sea battle

Jarl Erik [drew] the Iron Beard alongside the outermost of King Olaf's ships, thinned it of men, cut the cables, and let it drift free. Then he [drew] alongside the next, and fought until he had cleared it of men too.... At last it came to this, that all King Olaf's ships were cleared of men except the Long Serpent, on board of which gathered all who could still use their weapons. Then Iron Beard [drew] side-to-side with the Serpent and the fight went on with battle-axe and sword.

KING OLAF TRYGGVASON'S SAGA

Battles at sea are less common than battles on land. Warships with large crews cannot remain at sea for more than a few days, so it is impossible for one fleet to patrol the open sea in the hopes of intercepting a hostile fleet before it makes landfall. Very rarely, a merchant ship has been taken on the open sea, but full-scale battles between fleets usually take place in the sheltered and confined waters of a harbour, bay, fjord or river estuary, as at Hafrsfjord, where King Harald Fairhair won control of Norway around a hundred years ago.

Sinking enemy ships is not the point of a sea battle. Ships are valuable, so the idea is to capture them intact. In any case, longships do not carry any weapons capable of holing another ship below the waterline. Sea battles are fought in much the same way as land battles, but with the ships themselves forming the battlefield. The opposing fleets form up in line, prows-on to the other. The largest ships are stationed in the centre. Masts and sails are taken down before battle to clear the decks for action: all manoeuvring is done under oars alone.

The defending fleet may use the masts and spars to lash its ships together so that they form a solid fighting platform. This has the advantage that warriors can move quickly from ship to ship to where they are most needed. The attacking fleet may also do this, but only after it has made contact with the enemy fleet. Tactics are simple: use grappling hooks and anchors to fasten on to the enemy ships, try to board them, clear their decks in hand-to-hand fighting, cut them loose and then row them away.

Tips for a sea battle:

- Use horns to make pre-arranged signals.

- Use natural features to gain an advantage just as you would in land warfare. Anchoring the wings of a fleet against reefs or shoals protects it from outflanking. By deploying in a narrow inlet a smaller fleet can negate a larger fleet's advantage of numbers.

- In the early stages of the action, leave shields in their racks along the ship's gunwales to give the oarsmen some cover from missiles as the two fleets close in on one another.

- Always station the best warriors on the bows – they're the shipboard equivalent of the front rank of the shield wall on land.

- Leave a few small, fast ships free to patrol the flanks to cut out any ships trying to escape and to attack any men in the water who may be attempting to swim to the shore.

Size matters. The bigger a ship is the more men it can carry. Bigger ships are also taller. A high-sided ship gives better protection from missiles for its crew and it is harder for attackers to board. Its crew can in turn rain missiles down onto the crew of a smaller ship and are also more easily able to board it. Victory is likely to go to the side with the most large ships rather than the greatest number of ships overall.

Sea battles have all the risks of death and injury of a land battle plus the chance of drowning if you go over the side. Anyone wearing full mail armour will sink like a stone. It's not so much the weight of the mail itself that will drag you straight to the bottom, but the padded coat underneath, which immediately becomes waterlogged. Many warriors prefer to go without mail in a sea battle for this reason and because it's easier to row without a mail coat.

The Spoils of War

They sail near to the sea-shore so that they might claim for themselves the territories' plunder.

DUDO OF ST QUENTIN

× | × | × | × | × | × | × | × | ×

Payment for a Viking is strictly by results: no plunder means you don't get paid. All plunder is pooled and shared out according to the fellowship agreement, with the leader getting by far the largest share. This may seem unfair since all share the same dangers, but war leaders know that their warriors expect them to be generous gift givers and to supply them with good food and drink. They therefore do not keep their share of the plunder for long, as most of it is eventually given to their warriors in one form or another.

Holding back plunder is frowned upon. Not all members of a raiding party have an equal opportunity to loot as some must always be detailed for tasks like guarding the ships, reconnaissance, cutting off escape routes and such like. As these tasks are essential to the success of a raid, those who perform them must be rewarded equally with everyone else. If you keep back plunder for yourself you are dishonestly robbing your fellow Vikings.

Treasure

Treasure is what most Vikings dream of winning on a raid. Gold is the most desirable metal, but silver is much more plentiful both as jewelry and coins. Much that appears to be gold turns out to be only gold-plated silver. The custom with treasure is that it is all hacked to pieces

LEFT *Get your silver melted down and made into arm rings so that you can wear your wealth. No one can rob you without cutting your arms off, and you're not going to let anyone do that, are you?*

BELOW *Viking coins from Jorvik or Dublin. Coins can be handier for minor transactions than lumps of hacksilver, especially in countries like England and Frankia where their use is normal.*

so that it can be weighed and shared out more easily between the warriors. Sometimes it may be melted down and made into small ingots or arm rings. These last are a convenient and secure way to carry your loot around – and let people see that you're worth something at the same time. No particular value should be placed on the quality of the craftsmanship of an object, it's worth no more than what it weighs.

Coins

Gold coins are only commonly used in Mikligard, elsewhere they are made of silver. Coins are not in regular use for trade in the Scandinavian countries, so they are usually melted down like any other form of treasure to make ingots. However, they are a convenient size and weight for minor transactions, and they can easily be cut up into smaller pieces if necessary. Viking settlers in Ireland, England and Frankia are now completely accustomed to using coins like the locals.

The silver content of coins can vary considerably. Rulers can profit by manipulating the silver content of their coinage, for example by recalling coins with a high silver content, melting them down, holding back some of the silver for their treasury, and minting new coins with a higher proportion of base metal to silver. These may have the same nominal value and appearance as the old coins, but their lower silver content means that they are worth less. Be careful when dealing with traders, they are acutely aware of the real value of different coin issues and won't hesitate to take advantage of their knowledge. English pennies are heavier and have a higher silver content than Frankish deniers. A rough guide to the value of an English penny is that five will buy a sheep, ten a pig. Because of their relatively high value, forgeries, made of silver-plated copper, are common. Don't get caught out. You can easily detect these forgeries by scratching the surface of the coin with your knife.

Bulk commodities

Other forms of wealth, such as cloth, hides, ships, timber, grain and livestock, base metals and iron are less convenient to transport and share out, but they are readily converted into bullion by trading them with the merchants who are never far behind a successful Viking raiding party.

Slaves

People are among the most valuable spoils of war. Depending on their status, age, sex and health, they may be ransomed or sold as slaves. Slave trading requires a considerable investment of effort. Slaves must be guarded, so they don't escape, and fed and cared for to maintain their value. Chain slaves together by the neck for maximum security when taking them to market. Don't waste resources on elderly or infirm people who won't find a buyer; either kill them or let them go. Take especially good care of attractive young girls. Because they are desirable for sex they can easily fetch three times the price of a healthy male slave (10–11 ounces of silver). All nations keep slaves, but the biggest demand is from the Greeks, Moors and Saracens.

Viking men are not expected to be faithful to their wives. You are free to use any female slave you acquire on campaign for casual sex or as a longer-term concubine (if you are single, watch out, many a man has married a slave girl!). However, don't regard all slave girls as fair game. If you get caught having sex with another man's slave without having asked his permission first, you will have to pay him compensation for the use of his property. It is not illegal for you to kill your own slaves, any more than it is illegal for you to kill your own livestock, but should you kill another man's slave you will have to pay compensation equal to the full market value.

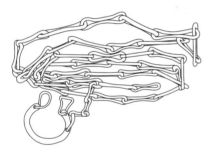

Protect your plunder. Use iron neck rings and chains to stop your slaves running away on their way to the market.

Ransom

Ransom has been a mainstay of Viking activity ever since the monks of Lindisfarne were carried off in 793. Almost anything can be ransomed, but it is high-status people who get the best prices. The record price was probably achieved in 858 for abbot Louis of the monastery of St Denis near Paris. His ransom was 686 pounds of gold and 3,250 pounds of silver. Given that gold is so much more valuable than silver (probably about 14 times more valuable), this was worth considerably more than the 10,000 pounds of silver King Aethelred paid Olaf

A reasonable man in a reasonable world. Just why are
people frightened of Vikings?

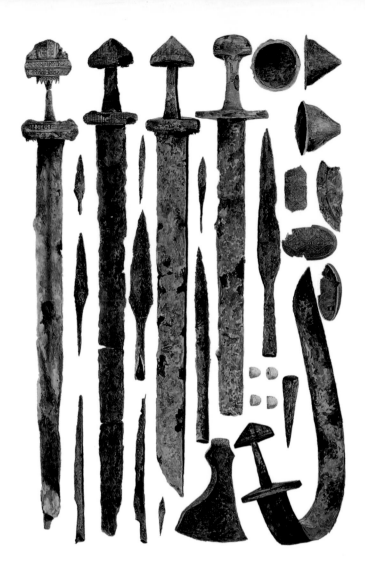

ABOVE It is customary to bury warriors with their weapons. Snapping or bending the swords, as here, makes sure that the dead warrior's ghost cannot use them against the living if it is at all unhappy with its treatment.

OPPOSITE Fighting on board ship isn't that different from fighting on land. You may still have to form a shield wall to repel boarders, like these spearmen.

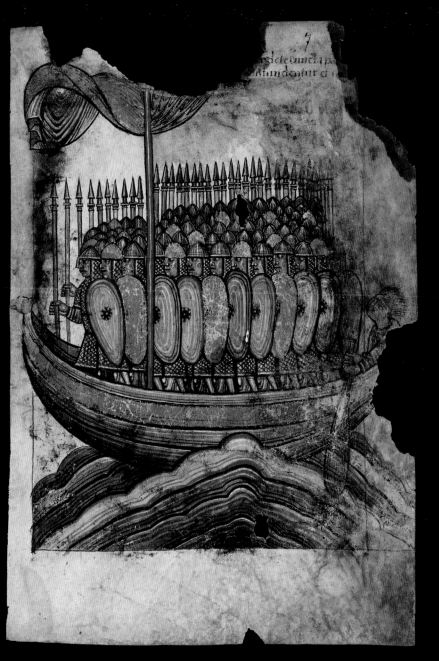

LEFT AND OPPOSITE Booty fit for a king. There are nearly 500 silver rings here, and that's only part of it: there are 14,000 silver coins from Serkland and much else besides. Whoever owned it buried it on Gotland, but never came back to recover it. The farmer who found it couldn't believe his luck.

BELOW A wealthy Rus lady's treasure hoard. The oval brooches come from Scandinavia, but her man probably looted the rest from the Slavs.

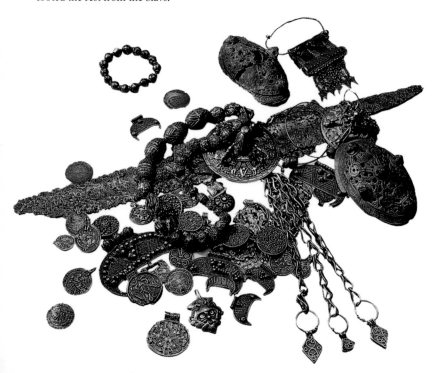

OPPOSITE ABOVE Normally Vikings just hack everything up to make sharing out the loot easier. This fine brooch must have taken some important man's fancy. He took it as his share and gave it to his Irish ladyfriend Melbrigda, who wrote her name on it in runes.

OPPOSITE BELOW Arm rings, made by melting down and recasting hacksilver, are a convenient way to carry and display your loot.

ABOVE LEFT Gotlanders know how to remember their dead. All over the island you'll see fine grave markers like this, with scenes of gods, battle and seafaring.

ABOVE RIGHT Woodcarving attracts the best artistic talent in Scandinavia. This great example shows the legendary smith Regin at work on the magical sword Gram.

ABOVE The chief's great hall. You're looking at it from the outside now, but become a Viking and you could be inside feasting with the chief at the high table.

BELOW Can't afford a real longship for your burial? No problem. Your family can just lay out a ship setting around your grave with stones. It's the thought that counts.

As a pagan Viking you may have little use for books, but the Christians value them and will pay handsomely for the return of expensive holy books. The scribble along the bottom of this page records how this book was ransomed from Vikings 150 years ago.

Tryggvason for peace last summer. Don't be downbeat if your captives don't include someone of this calibre, however. It is even possible to ransom serfs. Their lords need them to work their lands and will pay handsomely to get them back.

A degree of trust is necessary for successfully concluding the ransom of a hostage. It is generally thought to be wrong to kidnap and ransom people who have come to the camp to pay ransom for hostages. Nevertheless, it does happen that hostages are killed even though their ransom has been paid and, sometimes, people who have been promised safe conduct to deliver payments are themselves kidnapped and held to ransom. This sort of behaviour simply discourages people from paying ransoms and selfishly ruins business for straight-dealing Vikings.

It is important to remember that hostages are not slaves. They should be treated reasonably well unless ransom is not paid, in which case they can either be sold as slaves or, if they are old or unfit, killed. Christians put a high value on chastity in women and their families may disown female hostages if they have been raped. The same is true of the holy virgins called nuns. They are worth more if left intacto (even if you believe that in their profession they would be really grateful for a night in bed with a man).

Christians are also willing to pay well to recover holy objects looted from churches and monasteries. Sacred vessels can be redeemed for more than their value in bullion. Christians also greatly value holy books, and 'relics': the dry bones and desiccated body parts of holy men and women, which they childishly believe can work miracles. Relics are stored in caskets called reliquaries, which are usually made of precious metals and studded with jewels. Even church and domestic buildings can be held to ransom. The Vikings who sacked the Frankish port of Quentovic in 842 spared the houses of those people who paid ransom.

> *The monks of the abbey of Fontanelle ... were at this point in time [841]*
> *very frightened and terribly distressed. They seemed to be paralysed*
> *by uncertainty, rather than getting away with their lives. For they*
> *themselves had purchased the site of the monastery from the pagans at*
> *a good price. But when their funds had dried up and their immunity*
> *from attack was waning, they made up their minds, at the last moment,*
> *to embrace the safeguard of flight.*
>
> THE DISCOVERY AND MIRACLES OF ST VULFRAM

Tip Christian holy books are worth looting for their jewelled covers. Once you've ripped the jewels off, don't throw the pages away. They're made of vellum – calf skin – and can be cut up to make comfortable insoles for boots.

A Norwegian Viking stole this lovely reliquary from an Irish monastery and gave it to his girlfriend, Ranvaig, to use as a jewel box.

Scales, for weighing the loot and sharing it out fairly, are an essential part of a Viking leader's kit. Even coins are shared by weight, not by their nominal value.

Tribute

Even as a rank-and-file Viking, your share of one really big payment of tribute can be enough to set you up for life. Negotiations for a payment of tribute are most easily started after a decisive victory in battle when the enemy is very much on the back foot and desperately looking for ways to minimize their losses. Tribute can be collected in an orderly way, by local royal tax collectors, without the wider economic damage that would be the inevitable consequence of a Viking army rampaging freely over the countryside. It makes sense for the defeated party. It also makes sense for the Vikings, as someone else does their work for them and they don't have to take any risks themselves. In the west, tribute is usually demanded, and paid, in precious metals. In the Slav lands of the east, which do not have well-organized kingdoms like England and Frankia, tribute is usually taken in slaves, furs and other goods which have then to be traded with the Bulgars, Saracens or Greeks in order to convert them into bullion.

There is often a lot of bad faith shown by both sides during tribute negotiations. The enemy may spin out negotiations to buy time to raise fresh forces, gather the harvest in and remove it to safety, or wait for the onset of winter to bring campaigning to a natural end. The Vikings will promise peace – or even to go away and never return, ever – but paying tribute is a sign of weakness and Vikings find it hard to resist taking advantage of that. They'll be back and the tribute payers know it. In any respite given them after a payment of tribute they will be hoping to reorganize their defences and be in better shape to resist further attacks. It sometimes works out for them but not always. The one thing people everywhere expect from their kings is strong military leadership: when a king pays tribute, the people smell a rat. For a king who already has problems, like England's king Aethelred, paying tribute is likely to make them more unpopular, increase dissent, and further undermine the kingdom's defences. That's why the Vikings will be back in England next summer.

Negotiations Before the Battle of Brunanburh

[The messengers said] that it would be better for King Olaf to go back to Scotland and that as a gesture of friendship King Athelstan would give him a silver shilling for every plough in his kingdom, and in that way seal their relationship.... Once the message had been delivered Olaf put things off for the day and settled down for discussions with the leaders of his army. Opinions were sharply divided. Some urged him to accept the terms since the campaign had been highly successful and now they would go back with the load of tribute Athelstan was ready to hand over; but others were against it, arguing that if they were to reject this offer of Athelstan's, he would have to make a bigger one next time, and this is what they agreed.

EGIL'S SAGA

Ironically, the Vikings lost and so left with nothing.

In 845 Charles the Bald, king of the Franks
(r. 840–77), began the practice of paying tribute
to the Vikings in return for peace. It didn't work
for him and it isn't going to work for Aethelred
of England either.

Repudiating an agreement

Think very carefully before repudiating an agreement. If people get the idea that Vikings will always show bad faith, they won't negotiate in the first place. There should ideally always be some reason, no matter how specious, that allows you to present repudiating an agreement as an act of principle rather than the cynical opportunism that it really is. A fine example of this occurred early in 884 when King Carloman of the Franks agreed to pay the Vikings tribute of 12,000 pounds of gold and silver in return for leaving the kingdom. A truce, guaranteed by hostages, was agreed until October to deliver the money. However, shortly before the money was paid, Carloman died in a hunting accident. The Vikings claimed that their agreement had been a personal one with Carloman and said that if his successor wanted peace, he would have to pay them the same amount of money again; to drive the point home, they murdered the hostages and began plundering again.

Land

One of the great attractions of Viking raiding has always been grabbing some land. Many Vikings take their loot home and buy some land there, but plenty of others have made new lives for themselves on conquered lands overseas. Claiming land somewhere like Iceland was easy:

there was nobody there except for a few Irish monks and they cleared off pretty fast as soon as the first Viking ships showed up. However, most of the places that Vikings have settled were already inhabited and the locals weren't keen to make room for newcomers.

One effective way to secure land is to kill or expel the natives. This is what happened in Orkney and Shetland. Most of the local Pictish men were killed or sold as slaves, but most of the conquering Vikings were single men and they took the local women as wives and concubines. Problem solved, but the circumstances were special, they were isolated islands with small populations that had nowhere to hide: in most places this isn't possible.

A less bloodthirsty solution is to overthrow the native aristocracy and simply step into their shoes, taking over their lands and their authority. The native peasantry can be left with their lands, the only change for them being that they work for new Viking masters. So long as they are exploited no worse than they were by their previous masters, little trouble is to be expected from them.

No special effort is required to exterminate the native aristocracy either. As they will have formed the core of the defending armies, a large proportion of them will already have been killed in battle in the course of the conquest. This is very much what happened after the great Danish army invaded England in 865. The kings of East Anglia and Northumbria were killed in battle with a great many of their leading men and the king of Mercia fled into exile, leaving his kingdom demoralized and leaderless. With established authority in ruins, the Danes settled unopposed and set up their own kingdoms.

In Christian countries the church can be a willing collaborator even with pagan conquerors: it values peace and order above all, to protect its people, buildings and land. In the Danish kingdom of Jorvik, the local archbishops proved very helpful to their new pagan rulers, putting their administrative expertise at their disposal.

Land can be held more securely if possession can be recognized formally through negotiations with neighbouring powers. Even though they've now accepted English rule, the descendants of the Danes who conquered East Anglia are still there thanks to the frontier treaty their leader Guthrum negotiated with Alfred of Wessex in 886. Alfred recognized Danish possession of lands that had never belonged to Wessex anyway and got a settled frontier in return. Guthrum and his followers got a guarantee that Alfred wouldn't interfere while they consolidated their control over their conquests. When Alfred's son Edward conquered East Anglia in 917, the Danes were so well established that he let them keep their lands and laws.

Give him a piece of good land and your average Viking will gladly give up a life of violence and settle down. He'll even be happy to fit in with the way the locals do things, like Guthrum did when he became king of East Anglia: he adopted an English Christian name, 'Athelstan', and modelled his coins on King Alfred's.

The treaty between Hrolf the Ganger and the Frankish king Charles the Simple in 911 (see chapter 3) was mutually beneficial in the same way and has also lasted. By becoming Charles' vassal, Hrolf got legal title to the lands he had conquered on the Seine, while Charles gained recognition of his nominal rule over lands he didn't actually control. Guthrum and Hrolf both helped the negotiations along by converting to Christianity – this always pleases Christian rulers.

Where Vikings have not been able to reach agreements like these, they have struggled to hold on to lands they have conquered. This is especially true in Ireland where the Vikings scarcely control any land more than a spear's throw from the walls of their towns and, though they grow wealthy from trade, they live in a state of permanent insecurity.

– 10 –

The Sword's Sleep

Always keep in mind the day of death.

THE KING'S MIRROR

× | × | × | × | × | × | × | × | × | ×

A heroic death in battle is a fine thing, but most Vikings are in no great hurry to go to Valhalla. All true warriors do believe that it's better to be a dead lion than a live dog, but they also believe that it's still better to be a live lion than a dead one. However, war is a dangerous business and, win or lose, a Viking has a serious chance of being injured or killed. Should this happen to you, don't dishonour yourself and your family by howling in pain or by begging the enemy to spare your life. Injury and death must be faced with as much bravado and fatalistic indifference as you can manage.

Injury

A lot of sharp iron gets thrown around on a battlefield and you'll be lucky to escape completely unscathed. You'll hardly notice minor injuries like cuts and broken ribs while the battle frenzy is with you, and such wounds usually heal quickly by themselves afterwards. Any other kind of injury is seriously bad news. Treatment is generally painful and dangerous, often ineffective and very likely to make you wish you'd had a quick, clean, glorious death in battle. Wounds should be borne bravely, without any screaming or shouting out, but that's easier said than done.

Medicines, bone setting and surgery are usually the preserve of women. A good woman healer should also know the right runic charms

Odin rides his eight-legged stallion Sleipnir into Valhalla after a hard day's fighting with his einherjar. A Valkyrie offers him a refreshing cup of mead.

to promote healing and have the gift of healing hands. Hopefully, there will be at least one among the army's women followers. Their services don't come free of charge – you'll have to pay them for your treatment if you survive. If the army has no healers, choose the men with the softest hands to bandage wounds and tend to the injured.

First aid Cobwebs or waybread (greater plantain) applied to wounds helps stop bleeding and aids healing.

Stomach wounds Stomach wounds are almost always fatal if the bowels have been pierced. The time to get especially worried is if you're fed a strong-smelling leek or onion broth (that means they think the wound *is* that bad). If the wound later begins to smell of leeks it is a sign that your bowels have been pierced. Nothing can be done and you will develop a fever and die within two to three days.

Broken bones Broken legs and arms must be properly set by an expert if they are to heal straight. Bone setting is very painful, but it's worth the suffering because a broken leg or arm that mends crooked is not much use. The bone setter first spreads a salve of bonewort (daisy) and egg white on the broken limb before setting it in a splint. When a broken bone has not pierced through the skin, the patient can make a good recovery if the setter has done her job properly. If, as is often

Vikings don't always win. This bunch were captured by the English, bound and beheaded. Rest assured, they probably spat in the executioner's eye.

the case with injuries inflicted with swords and axes, the flesh has been cut open and bone has been exposed to the air and dirt, the patient usually dies of fever before the bone has knit. In these circumstances the best choice is to amputate the limb immediately, which often kills the patient anyway.

Bleeding Deep cuts and wounds are best treated by cauterization with a red-hot iron. This stops the bleeding and cleans the wound at the same time. Gaping wounds and the stumps of severed limbs may need to be sewn up. Sewing needles are made of bone and are not sharp enough to pierce the skin. The healer prepares the wound for stitching by boring a series of holes in the flesh using a sharp metal probe: only then can it be sewn up using a needle and linen thread (or silk, if you can afford it). Applying salt and leek leaves to a wound before treatment helps to the dull the pain. A salve of silverweed, springwort (spurge), groundsel, sengreen (houseleek), woodruff and wormwood boiled in butter helps heal any wound made by iron.

Arrow wounds Arrows cause some of the most unpleasant injuries going. The arrows used for fighting are sharply barbed such that they cannot be pulled out of a wound without causing a lot more damage. If the arrow has not penetrated too deeply, the healer will cut the flesh around the wound so that it can be pulled out. She will then clean the wound, removing any splinters, before cauterizing it. If the arrow has penetrated deeply, it is often less damaging to cut off the fletched end and push the arrow right through the body so that it comes out the other side. If there is a bone in the way, it is necessary to break it first so that the arrow can be pushed through. After cleaning, both wounds are cauterized. Don't expect to enjoy the experience.

War fetter (*herfjöttr*) After a battle, you may find some men wandering around the battlefield dazed and confused by the shock and violence of combat. They are suffering from 'war fetter' or 'foot terror'. With rest and gentle treatment they will recover their wits eventually.

> *Thormod went into a house where there were many wounded men, and with them a young woman binding their wounds.... The girl said, 'Let me see your wound and I will bind it.' Thormod sat down and took off his clothes. The girl examined the wound – it was in his side – and felt that there was an iron arrowhead in it but could not find where it had gone in. In a stone pot she boiled a mixture of leeks and other herbs and gave it to the wounded men to eat. By this she discovered if the wounds had penetrated the gut, for if the wound had gone so deep it would smell of leeks. She brought some of this to Thormod and told him to eat it. He replied 'Take it away, I've no appetite for broth.' Then she took a pair of tongs and tried to pull out the arrowhead but it was stuck fast and would not come out. As the wound was swollen, little of it stood out to take hold of. Now Thormod said, 'Cut deep enough so that you can get at the arrowhead with the tongs, then give me them to me and let me pull.' She did as he said. Then Thormod took a gold ring from his fingers and gave it to the girl and told her do with it as she liked. 'It was the gift of a good man,' he said, 'King Olaf gave it me this morning.' Then Thormod took the tongs and pulled the arrowhead out. On the barbs there hung some pieces of flesh from his heart, some white, some red. When he saw that, he said 'See how well the king feeds his men; there is fat around my heart,' and saying this he leant back and died.*
>
> SAINT OLAF'S SAGA

Death in battle

Your comrades are celebrating a great victory, but you didn't see that big English axeman until it was too late and now you're dead. What comes next? Who knows for sure? Every year more people are converting to the new Christian religion and Denmark even has a Christian king. However, if you are a true Viking warrior you will surely remain loyal to the old religion with its promise, to those who die in battle, of a glorious afterlife of feasting and fighting with the All Father Odin in Valhalla (the 'hall of the slain').

Odin regards killing or being killed in battle as equally praiseworthy. Odin is informed of all developments by his ravens Hugin and Mumin who fly out over the world and return to whisper what they have learned in his ears. When he hears that warriors are advancing on one another to do glorious battle, he despatches the Valkyries, his battle-maidens, to decide who will be slain and who will live. After the battle the Valkyries conduct the souls of the fallen warriors to Odin's hall Valhalla in Asgard, the home of the gods. There they are welcomed

by the poet-god Bragi, whose duty it is to prepare Valhalla for their arrival. Valhalla is a vast hall, so vast that hammer-wielding Thor's own hall lies inside it. Valhalla shines with gold, has great spears for rafters and is roofed with shields and mail coats. There are 540 doors, each so large that 800 warriors can exit from them abreast.

LEFT *Odin with his ravens Hugin and Mumin who bring him news of strife in the world.*

ABOVE *Odin's shield-maidens, the Valkyries, welcome the slain warriors into Valhalla.*

The destiny of the slain is to join the ranks of the *einherjar*, Odin's personal warrior retinue. Every morning the *einherjar* pour out of Valhalla and spend the day battling one another. In the evening, the fallen are restored to life and the wounded are healed in time to spend the night feasting on roast boar and drinking the finest mead with the gods while being waited on by beautiful Valkyries.

Admission to this warrior paradise does not depend on any special treatment for the warrior's corpse. This is a comfort to the warrior who is killed far from home, especially if he fights on the losing side and is left unburied on the battlefield for the wolves and carrion birds to squabble over. However, Odin has decreed that any fallen warrior who is cremated can take to Valhalla all of the weapons and other goods that are placed on the pyre with him. There is no more equality in the afterlife than in this one.

Ragnarok: the final battle

All good things come to an end sooner or later and not even the afterlife is forever. Odin is gathering his warriors for a purpose – to fight with him and his fellow gods against their ancient enemies, the giants and their allies, at Ragnarok, the final battle at the end of time. Unfortunately, there will be no boasting in the mead hall afterwards because Odin and his warrior *einherjar*, are fated to be annihilated along with their enemies. Flames hurled by the fire giant Surt will burn the earth completely before it sinks below the waves of the sea, one day to re-emerge purified to begin a new cycle of the universe.

Alternative afterlives

> *The foolish man thinks he will live forever,*
> *If he keeps away from fighting;*
> *But old age won't grant him a truce*
> *Even if the spears do.*
>
> HÁVAMÁL

Only berserkers are actually eager to die in battle so that they can join the *einherjar* as quickly as possible. For most rational Vikings, entering Valhalla is only a consolation for death in battle; what they really want to do is to live and enjoy the fruits of victory. But no one can escape death. While the warrior who dies in battle is guaranteed a glorious afterlife, the soul roads taken by those who die of illness, old age or drowning are many, and not all of them are good.

For the most part, the souls of the dead linger on in a ghostly afterlife in their graves, comforted by whatever offerings their families could afford to bury with them. Who would envy the lot of a slave sacrificed to accompany his or her master in death? Yet some volunteer. The souls of the righteous may be lucky enough to find their way to Brimir, a golden-roofed hall in the region of the otherworld called Gimlé: they will be served good ale there. Or perhaps they will go instead to another hospitable hall, Sindri in the otherworld's Niðafjöll mountains. In this way a great warrior may still find an abode with the gods even if he does not die in battle. The souls of unwed girls are claimed by the licentious fertility goddess Freyja who takes them to dwell in her own realm of Fólkvangr. Odin allows Freyja to take a share of his warriors to dwell in Fólkvangr to keep them company: if you died expecting to enter Valhalla you might not feel too disappointed if you are one of them.

Death by drowning is an obvious risk for a Viking warrior. The souls of the drowned are in for a soggy afterlife under the sea in the hall of the sea god Aegir whose wife Rán snares them in her net. Aegir has a reputation for being the best brewer among the gods, so it's not a bad fate.

The other roads for the souls of those who die of illness or old age are rather gloomy. Some will find their way to the freezing fog-realm of Niflheim where they will share the meagre fare offered by the decaying goddess Hel. Oath breakers and murderers have the miserable time they deserve in Nástrandir, a frightful hall made of woven serpents, dripping with venom. The most wicked souls are cast into the well of Hvergelmir, to be fed on by the serpent Niðhöggr, the corpse-tearer.

Treatment of the dead

It is customary to treat the enemy dead with disrespect. After robbing them of all their valuables, toss their bodies carelessly into a mass grave or, if that seems like too much trouble, simply leave them for the wolves, ravens and other carrion feeders to dispose of. Get killed fighting on the losing side of a battle and this will happen to you. If circumstances allow, Viking dead should be treated with the same respect they would get at home. Warriors who believe in the old gods should be buried with their weapons in a wooden coffin or a timber-lined chamber. For a chieftain, the ideal send-off is a ship burial with grave offerings appropriate to his status – weapons, treasure, a slave girl, and maybe horses and hunting dogs.

There's not really a lot of agreement about what to do next. Bury everything under a barrow, burn everything and then bury it under a barrow, set the ship adrift on the open sea, or set fire to the ship and set it adrift on the open sea? They've all been done. For the less wealthy, such as a minor chief, burial in a rowing boat is an acceptable substitute for a ship. The closest to a ship burial the rest can hope for is to be buried with a few old hull planks or in a grave surrounded by boulders laid out in the shape of a longship: it's the thought that counts.

The dead are never gone forever and, if they are unhappy, their ghosts may wander and cause trouble for the living. Troublesome ghosts must be disabled by cutting off their corpse's head and feet or by scattering the bones. As an additional precaution, break all the grave goods too, especially weapons, so that the dead cannot use them.

A real warrior's burial. With the sword, axe, spears, arrows, shields and the two horses that were buried with him, this man would have cut a dash when he arrived in the afterlife.

Surrender

> *A man was brought out to be executed and Thorkel [asked him what*
> *he thought about dying]. He said, 'I think well of death, as do all of us.*
> *But I am not minded to be slaughtered like a sheep, and would rather*
> *face the blow. You hew into my face and watch closely if I flinch.' ...*
> *They did what he asked for and let him face the blow. Thorkel stepped*
> *in front of him and hewed into his face; and he did not flinch a whit*
> *except that his eyes closed when death came upon him.*
>
> THE SAGA OF THE JÓMSVÍKINGS

Surrender is never a good option, but if your comrades are dead or fled, your shield is shattered and your sword blunt, there is a slim chance it might save your life and buy time while you look for an opportunity to escape. If your enemy is in a bad mood, as people often are if they've just seen a lot of their friends get killed, they will probably just cut you down on the spot anyway. If, however, the battle frenzy has begun to wear off and they're getting sick of killing, you may be spared while they decide what to do with you.

If you're a survivor of a small raiding party you shouldn't hold out much hope. Since ancient times, it has always been the custom everywhere to execute pirates, so you will probably quickly be hanged or beheaded. Otherwise, your best hope of survival is that your captors will ransom you if you are noble, or sell you into slavery if you are not. If you're very lucky, if you fought well and showed unflinching bravery, you may be invited to sign on as a mercenary with your captor's army. Don't worry that you might be thought a traitor. If your lord was killed in the fight, you are now free to fight for whomever you like without dishonour.

OPPOSITE *A runestone erected to the memory of the Swedish warrior Geirfastr who was killed fighting in England. He died well and made his family proud. They erected this stone so that even in a thousand years' time people will still speak his name when less brave men are long forgotten.*

Tip If captured by Christians, try offering to convert. Christians believe that persuading other people to follow their religion is pleasing to their god, so this may save your life. New converts are often given gifts too, so you won't go home completely empty-handed (the downside is that you have to let a priest pour water over your head first). Some Vikings are known to have been converted more than once in this way.

The end

If you are to be executed it is important to show no fear and to treat the loss of your life as if it is of no great consequence even to you. This will earn you the respect of your captors and enhance your posthumous reputation if word gets back to your family and friends. Do not dishonour yourself by begging for your life. If you are to be beheaded, it is a particularly impressive act of bravado to tell your executioner to strike at your neck from the front, rather than from behind. This way you can look him in the eye fearlessly while he swings his sword or axe. Don't flinch at the last moment – this will spoil the effect. Witty insults are also highly regarded because they show that you've kept your presence of mind in the face of imminent death. This is your last chance to make a good impression, don't waste it.

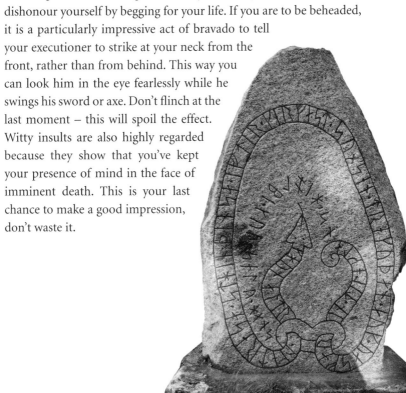

*Some of the offerings from the Swedish warrior burial
shown on p. 191.*

to Greenland

ICELAND

N

FAEROES

SHETLAND

WESTERN

OCEAN

SUDREYS

ORKNEY

NORWAY

SWEDEN

Birka

GOTLAND

Iona

SCOTLAND

NORTH

JUTLAND

EASTERN SEA

Armagh

IRELAND

Lindisfarne

SEA

DENMARK

WENDLAND

Dublin

Jorvik

Hedeby

WALES

Maldon

FRISIA

ENGLAND

Dorestad

Portland

FLANDERS

Rouen

Seine

Chartres

Paris

Rhine

Loire

FRANKIA

MOORS

Córdoba

NARVESUND

Rome

MOORS

MIDDLE

0	500	1000 km

0	500 miles

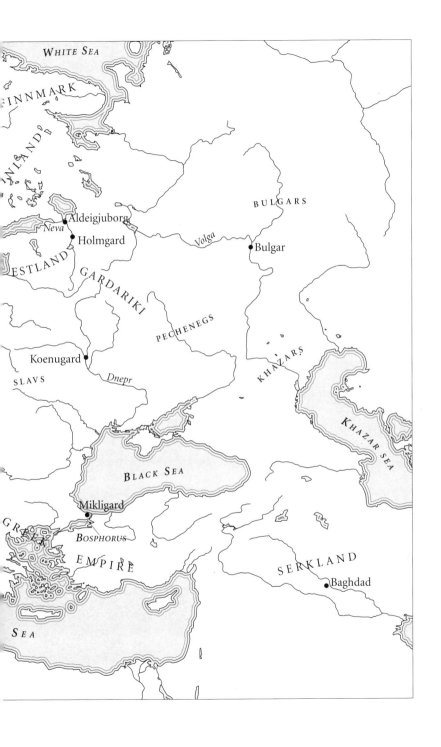

Glossary

Asgard home of the gods

berserkers Viking warriors that built themselves up into a trancelike state, which often gave them superhuman strength

Birka Swedish trading centre situated on an island near Stockholm

burh English town (hence Brunanburh, site of a Viking–English battle)

byrnie mail shirt

Danegeld tribute paid to Vikings in return for peace

Danelaw Danish-occupied land in the east of England

drakkar large Viking warship; its name means 'dragon'

druzhina a Rus king's warrior retinue

ealdorman English lord, roughly equivalent to a jarl

Eastern Sea the Baltic Sea

einherjar Odin's warrior retinue, made up from those slain in battle

flyting ritual exchange of insults, normally at a feast

Frankia in 991, the kingdom of France; earlier in the Viking Age, the Carolingian empire founded by the Frankish ruler Charlemagne, comprising modern France, the Low Countries, western Germany, Switzerland, Austria and Italy

Freyja the Norse goddess of sensual pleasure and fertility

futhark the Viking runic alphabet, named after its first six letters

Gardariki ('Land of Forts' or 'Land of Cities') European Russia

Greek empire the Byzantine (or Eastern Roman) empire

hafvilla losing one's bearings at sea

hersir a local lord – the lowest rank of the Scandinavian aristocracy in the Viking Age

hirð the warrior retinue of a powerful chieftain or king

hnefatafl a game played on a checkered board with two sets of counters of unequal strength. The objective of the game was for the player with the larger set to capture the 'king' piece of the weaker set

hólmganga duel held on an island to settle a dispute or offence

Holmgard Novgorod, Russia

housecarl bodyguard or retainer to a Viking lord or king

jarl 'earl', a regional lord, second only to the king in power

Jorvik York, England

Khazar Sea the Caspian Sea, named for the Khazars, a Turkic nomad people who settled on the steppes north of the sea in the 7th century

knattleitr a popular team game involving the use of wooden bats and a hard ball: the rules are not known, but it was very rough and players were often injured

Koenugard Kiev, Ukraine

levy conscripted army or warband called upon in time of crisis

Maldon (battle) victory of Olaf Tryggvason over the English ealdorman Byhrtnoth in 991

Middle Sea the Mediterranean Sea

Mikligard ('Great City') Constantinople (modern Istanbul), capital of the Byzantine empire

Moors Berber peoples of North Africa who also settled in southern Spain following the Islamic conquest in 711

Narvesund the Straits of Gibraltar

niðing 'nothing' – the name for a disgraced or disowned Viking

Njord god of sailors

Norns female deities whose role was to determine the fate of every human being, the gods, and the universe

Odin the chief god of the Norse pantheon, particularly associated with kingship, war, poetry and knowledge of runes

Pechenegs a Turkic nomad people who dominated the Ukrainian steppes in the 9th–11th centuries

portage dragging a ship across land; *see* pp. 91–92

Ragnarok the battle at the end of time

runes early Germanic writing system thought to be derived from the Latin and Etruscan alphabets, but according to Norse mythology invented by Odin

Rus term used to describe Scandinavians living in Russia, which is named for them, but probably derived from *Ruotsi*, the Finnish name for the Swedes

saga medieval Icelandic prose narrative literature

Serkland (meaning uncertain) the Arab Abbasid caliphate

shield wall formation of warriors in a line holding their shields in front of them; *see* p. 71

skald bard or court poet

snekke small Viking warship; its name means 'snake'

strandhogg hit-and-run raiding along a country's coastline

Sudreys the Hebridean islands off Scotland's west coast, from a Viking perspective, the 'South Isles'

thegn in Viking Age England, a local lord, roughly equivalent to a hersir

thing a regular assembly of freemen at which issues of law and politics were decided. There was a hierarchy of things at district, provincial and national levels

Thor the Norse god of physical strength, oaths, thunder and lightning, rain and good weather. He defended the gods and humans with his mighty hammer Mjöllnir

thrall slave

Valhalla 'the hall of the slain': Odin's hall where the souls of warriors slain in battle spent the afterlife feasting and fighting

Valkyries supernatural female warriors who dwelt with Odin in Valhalla

Varangian term used from the mid-10th century by the Slavs, Greeks and Arabs to describe Scandinavian mercenaries and traders newly arrived in the east from their homelands. The term is thought to be derived from Old Norse *vár* ('pledge'), possibly because bands of Scandinavian warriors and merchants formed sworn fellowships. The Varangian Guard were the Byzantine emperor's elite bodyguard

Wendland the country of the Wends, a group of Slavic peoples who, in the Viking Age, inhabited the south coast of the Baltic Sea between the neck of the Jutland peninsula and the mouth of the Vistula

Western Ocean Atlantic Ocean

Acknowledgments

The author wishes to thank Kim Siddorn, Steve Etheridge and Richard Walsh of the Regia Anglorum re-enactment group for sharing their practical insights into Viking life and times. Thanks also to William Short for giving permission to use his photographs of re-enactors demonstrating Viking combat techniques. At Thames & Hudson, Alice Reid has been a patient and constructive editor and Maria Ranauro has done an excellent job of the picture research. Rowena Alsey designed the layout.

Further Reading

Scandinavians of the Viking Age used runes to make short inscriptions on wood, stone and metal objects, but they did not have a fully literate culture until after their conversion to Christianity between the late 10th and early 12th centuries. The most vivid accounts of Viking Age warfare are to be found in the Icelandic sagas but it must always be borne in mind that, for all their convincing detail and realistic style, these were not written down until the 13th century, two to three hundred years after the events they describe. The family sagas should be read as historical novels based on the lives of real people and real events rather than as family history. The kings' sagas are historical biographies based in large part on orally transmitted skaldic verse, which is often quoted at length. The skalds' job was to glorify the deeds of their patrons, so their poems are not impartial sources, but, as they were often present at the battles they describe, they are still the nearest thing we have to eyewitness accounts of Viking warfare. Viking raids feature prominently in contemporary annals and chronicles compiled in Christian Europe, such as the *Anglo-Saxon Chronicle*, but generally do not include detailed accounts of battles.

The most important of the kings' sagas are contained in Snorri Sturluson's mighty *Heimskringla* ('The Circle of the World'), an epic history of the kings of Norway from legendary times until the death of Magnus IV in 1177. The most recent complete translation still in print is *Heimskringla: History of the Kings of Norway*, by Lee M. Hollander (University of Texas Press, 1964). Samuel J. Laing's translation of *Heimskringla*, originally published in 1844, is still very readable (although the translations of skaldic verse now seem very old-fashioned) and is available from several publishers as an e-book.

The most warlike of the Icelandic family sagas is *Egil's Saga*, based on the life of Egil Skallagrímsson, a 10th-century warrior, skald, merchant and farmer, whose adventures take him across much of the Viking world. The most readily available translation is by Herman Pálsson and Paul Edwards (Penguin Classics, 1976).

The Saga of the Jómsvíkings (trans. Lee M. Hollander, University of Texas Press, 1955) is about the exploits of the Jómsvíkings, a possibly fictitious band of elite Vikings who are supposed to have been active in the Baltic Sea at the end of the 10th century.

The Saga of the Volsungs: The Norse Epic of Sigurd the Dragon Slayer (trans. Jesse L. Byock, Hisarlik Press, 1993) is the most important of the legendary sagas and includes many descriptions of weapons, including the forging of the magical sword Gram, and of battles.

Translations of contemporary annals

The Anglo-Saxon Chronicles, trans Michael Swanton (Dent, 1996).
The Annals of St-Bertin, trans. Janet L. Nelson (Manchester University Press, 1991).
The Viking Age: A Reader, ed. Angus A. Somerville and R. Andrew McDonald (University of Toronto Press, 2010). Translated extracts from contemporary annals and other sources covering all aspects of Viking life.

Although composed from the Anglo-Saxon point of view, the Old English epic poem, *The Battle of Maldon,* recounting the last stand of ealdorman Byrhtnoth's household warriors in their battle against Olaf Tryggvason's Vikings in 991, gives important insights into warrior ideals of the period: see *Anglo-Saxon Poetry,* edited and translated by S. J. Bradley (Dent, 1982).

Secondary sources

The following books are good secondary sources, providing the reader with a broad introduction to Viking weapons and warfare and to their military campaigns:

Griffith, Paddy, *The Viking Art of War* (Greenhill, 1995).
Harrison, Mark, *Viking Hersir 793–1066* (Osprey, 1993).
Haywood, John, *The Penguin Historical Atlas of the Vikings* (Penguin, 1995).
Short, William R., *Viking Weapons and Combat Techniques* (Westholme, 2009).
Siddorn, J. Kim, *Viking Weapons and Warfare* (Tempus, 2000).

Sources of Quotations

6, 18, 54, 73, 140, 184 *The King's Mirror* (trans. L. M. Larson), New York: Twayne, 1917.
7, 127, 180 'Hávamál' in *The Poetic Edda* (trans. Carolyne Larrington), Oxford: OUP, 1996.
8, 29, 161 *Orkneyinga Saga* (trans. Hermann Pálsson and Paul Edwards), London: Hogarth Press, 1978.
10 Snorri Sturluson, 'St Olaf's Saga' in *Heimskringla* (trans. Samuel Laing), 1844, repr. London: J. M. Dent, 1915.
25 Sven Aggesen, 'The Law of the Retainers' in *The Works of Sven Aggesen* (trans. Eric Christiansen), London: The Viking Society for Northern Research, 1992.
27 Snorri Sturluson, 'Háttatal' in *Edda* (trans. Antony Faulkes), London: J. M. Dent, 1987.
30 'The Battle of Maldon' in *Anglo-Saxon Poetry* (trans. S. A. J. Bradley), London: J. M. Dent, 1982.
33 Snorri Sturluson, 'Ynglinga Saga' in *Heimskringla* (trans. Samuel Laing), 1844, repr. London: J. M. Dent, 1915.
35 *Laxdaela Saga* (trans. Magnus Magnusson and Hermann Pálsson), Harmondsworth: Penguin, 1969.

41 *Arrow Odd's Saga*, (trans. H. Pálsson and P. Edwards in Seven Viking Romances) Penguin, 1975.

43, 162 Snorri Sturluson, 'King Olaf Tryggvason's Saga' in *Heimskringla* (trans. Samuel Laing), 1844, repr. London: J. M. Dent, 1915.

47, 96, 165 Dudo of St Quentin (trans. Felice Lifshitz), ORB Online Library, http://www.the-orb.net/orb_done/dudo/dudindex.html.

53 Dudo of St Quentin, trans. in E. van Houts, *The Normans in Europe*, Manchester: Manchester University Press, 2000.

55 *The Saga of Grettir the Strong* (trans. G. A. Hight), London: Dent, 1914.

56, 150 *The Saga of the Volsungs* (trans. Jesse L. Byock), Oxford: OUP, 1996.

59, 94 'The Lay of Sigrdrifa' in *The Poetic Edda* (trans. Carolyne Larrington), Oxford: OUP, 1996.

62 Snorri Sturluson, 'Saga of Magnus the Blind and Harald Gille' in *Heimskringla* (trans. Samuel Laing), 1844, repr. London: J. M. Dent, 1915.

64 'Saga of the Vápnsfirðings', *Eirik the Red and other Icelandic Sagas* (trans. Gwyn Jones), Oxford: OUP, 1966.

64, 99 Saxo Grammaticus, *History of the Danes* (ed. H. Ellis Davidson, trans. P. Fisher), Woodbridge: D. S. Brewer, 1996.

74 Snorri Sturluson, 'St Olaf's Saga' in *Heimskringla* (trans. C. J. Laing), 1844, repr. London: J. M. Dent, 1915.

78 'The Seafarer' in *Anglo-Saxon Poetry* (trans. S. A. J. Bradley), London: J. M. Dent, 1982.

93, 156, 180 *Egil's Saga* (trans. Hermann Pálsson and Paul Edwards), Harmondsworth: Penguin, 1977.

101 William of Malmesbury, *Chronicles of the Kings of England* (trans. J. A. Giles), London: 1847.

104 Gerald of Wales, *The History and Topography of Ireland* (trans. J. J. O'Meara), Harmondsworth: Penguin, 1982.

108 Snorri Sturluson, 'The Saga of King Magnus Barefoot', in *Heimskringla* (trans. Samuel Laing), 1844, repr. London: J. M. Dent, 1915.

110 Gerald of Wales, *The Description of Wales* (trans. L. Thorpe), Harmondsworth, Penguin, 1978.

111 Anna Comnena, *The Alexiad* (trans. E. R. A. Sewter), Harmondsworth: Penguin, 1969.

115 Rimbert, 'The Life of St Anskar', trans. in Charles H. Robinson, *Anskar, the Apostole of the North, 801–865*, London: SPCK, 1921.

117 Snorri Sturluson, 'King Harald's Saga' in *Heimskringla* (trans. Samuel Laing), 1844, repr. London: J. M. Dent, 1915.

120 Trans. in Sigfús Blöndal, *The Varangians of Byzantium*, Cambridge: CUP, 1978.

123 Liudprand of Cremona, 'The Embassy to Constantinople' in *The Works of Liudprand of Cremona* (trans. F. A. Wright), London: Routledge, 1930.

124 Annals of St-Bertin, 844 (trans. J. L. Nelson), Manchester: Manchester University Press, 1991.

129, 132 Annals of Fulda, 891 (trans. Timothy Reuter), Manchester: Manchester University Press, 1992.

137 'Reginsmál' in *The Poetic Edda* (trans. Carolyne Larrington), Oxford: OUP, 1996.

155 'Royal Frankish Annals 820', trans. in B. W. Scholz, *Carolingian Chronicles*, Ann Arbor: University of Michigan, 1972.

161 *Annals of Ireland*, 918 (trans. John O'Donovan), Dublin, 1860.

178 'The Discovery and Miracles of St Vulfram', trans. in E. van Houts, *The Normans in Europe*, Manchester: Manchester University Press, 2000.

187 Snorri Sturluson, 'St Olaf's Saga' in *Heimskringla* (trans. Samuel Laing), 1844, repr. London: J. M. Dent, 1915.

189 'Hávamál' in *The Poetic Edda* (trans. Carolyne Larrington), Oxford: OUP, 1996.

192 *The Saga of the Jómsvíkings* (trans. Lee M. Hollander), Texas: University of Texas Press, 1955.

Sources of Illustrations

a = above; c = centre; b = below; l = left; r = right

Abbey of San Paolo Fuori le Mura/Istituto Poligrafico e Zecca dello Stato, Rome 181; Academy of Sciences, St Petersburg 119; Antikvarisk-Topografiska Arkivet, Stockholm 37, 77, 96, 133, 191, 194; Århus Museum 60ar; Bayeux Tapestry Museum, Normandy 7, 63al, 65, 71, 73, 114bl, 134, 143, 153, 154, 158; Berga, Sweden 193; Biblioteca Nacional de España. Skylitzes Matritensis 36, 39, 123; Biblioteca Nacional de España. Skylitzes Matritensis. Photo Album/Oronoz/AKG 15; Bibliothèque Nationale de France, Paris 171; Bodleian Library, Oxford 121; From M. Brisbane, *Archaeology of Novgorod*, Lincoln 1992 118; British Library, London 149; British Museum, London 1, 4, 5, 9, 11, 27r, 34, 64, 102, 156, 183; John Byford 188a; Dan Carlsson. Gotlands Museum, Visby, Sweden 172a, 173; Photo © Ted Spiegel/Corbis 176b; County Museum of Gotland, Sweden 166a; C. M. Dixon 55; Richard Hall 145, 188b; John Haywood 176a; Historisk Museum, Universitetet I Bergen 127; Hunterian Museum, Glasgow 50; Lindisfarne Holy Island, Northumberland 14; From Olaus Magnus, *Historia de Gentibus Septentrionalibus*, Rome 1555 16, 23, 92, 100, 162; Manx National Heritage, Douglas, Isle of Man 166b; Museo de Burgos. Photo Album/Oronoz/AKG 125; Museum of London 63ar; Museum of Cultural History, University of Oslo 66, 68, 69, 76, 78b, 95b, 175r; National Library, Stockholm 177; National Museum of Denmark, Copenhagen 57r, 63b, 170, 178; National Museum of Ireland, Dublin 139a; National Museum of Scotland, Edinburgh 174a; National Museums & Galleries of Wales, Cardiff 174b; Norwich Castle Museum 60arc, 95ac, 95ar; From E. Nylén and J. P. Lamm, *Bildstenar*, Gidlunds, Visby 1987 31l; Photo © Oxford Archaeology 186; Pierpont Morgan Library, New York 19; St. Paul im Lavanttal Library, Carinthia, Austria 112; State Hermitage Museum, St Petersburg 22, 172b; Statens Historiska Museum, Stockholm 13, 24, 27l , 31r, 42, 53, 60al–ar, 60b, 95al, 128, 137, 185; Photo © The Irish Image Collection/SuperStock 107; Photo © PhotoAlto/SuperStock 175l; After Svendsen 98; Drawing © Thames & Hudson Ltd, London 58, 114a, 139b, 141; Drawing by Lesley Collett © Thames & Hudson Ltd, London 131; Drawing by Nick Jakins © Thames & Hudson Ltd, London 29, 43, 49, 109, 168; Trinity College Library, Dublin 106; Upplandsmuseet, Uppsala 44; Illustration Morten Gøthche © The Viking Ship Museum, Denmark 74, 75; Photo Werner Karrasch © The Viking Ship Museum, Denmark 81–83; Viking Ship Museum, Bygdøy. Museum of Cultural History, University of Oslo 2, 3, 46, 89; Werner Forman Archive 78a; Werner Forman Archive/Viking Ship Museum, Bygdøy 169; Wikinger Museum, Haithabu 136; From William R. Short, *Viking Weapons and Combat Techniques*, Westerholme Publishing 2009. Courtesy hurstwic.org 56, 57l, 61, 84–88; York Archeological Trust 54, 138, 179.

Index